Praise for Lu

"You'll never look at the moon the same way again after reading *Lunar Alchemy*. Author Shaheen Miro encourages you to understand lunar phases in connection with the phases in your own life. The moon, he points out, is your mirror, and, like the moon, you're always changing. Are you waxing, waning, new, full? Miro shows you how to recognize the phase you're experiencing at any given time, align yourself with cosmic energy, and make the best of whatever cycle you're in. With the moon as your guide, you can embrace your personal ebbs and flows. He provides dozens of easy-to-do but powerful exercises, meditations, spells, and rituals designed to shift your perceptions so the 'luminous you' can come forth. Engaging and insightful, gracefully written and beautifully designed, *Lunar Alchemy* takes you on a journey of transformation that brings moon magic into every area of your life."

—Skye Alexander, author of *Magickal Astrology* and
The Modern Witchcraft Book of Tarot

"Like the phases of the moon, life is always in flux. When you learn how to lean into this flow, your life can become magical. In *Lunar Alchemy*, Shaheen Miro shows how to initiate transformation by following the cycles of the moon. This isn't your typical 'moon magic' book. While most books in that genre focus solely on manifestation and wish-making, *Lunar Alchemy* shines the light on the inner work first, helping the reader tap into the dark to find the gold. Rituals, exercises, and journaling prompts, all delivered in Shaheen's beautiful prose, set the stage for deep exploration and lasting change. Once you've worked through the inner alchemy, you're ready to make magic happen with spells and ceremonies that pave the way for creating the beautiful life you want."

—Theresa Reed, author of *Astrology for Real Life*

"In *Lunar Alchemy*, Miro offers an exciting entrance to the Hermetic path of working with cosmic rhythms to expand our daily experience of magic. This is the kind of work that can take you far outside your previous notions of who you are and into a joyful relationship with your own divine power. Miro guides readers through the strange paradoxes of the Moon's mirror with a confident hand and accessible practices. Don't hesitate to pick up this delightful book, run with its beauty, and amplify your magic in the world."

—Carolyn Elliott, author of *Existential Kink*

"As our understanding of the Moon becomes greater, so does our interest in how she can guide and transform our lives, phase by phase. In *Lunar Alchemy*, we are invited to form an intimate relationship with the Moon through ritual and exercises. This book acts as an alluring portrait of both her and her cycles but also is a hands-on manual for the everyday practitioner wishing to integrate the wisdom of this celestial body into their life."

—Steven Bright, author of *In Focus Tarot* and *Spirit Within Tarot*

"As a practicing witch for two decades and a devoted moonchild, I found myself completely spellbound by *Lunar Alchemy*! Filled with tips, tricks, exercises, and spells, Shaheen Miro's friendly and encouraging voice tenderly lifts readers from the book's pages and takes them on a magical journey to mother moon. Miro's teachings envelop the reader with enchantment in accordance to the wax and wane of the celestial cycles and tides of life—reminding us that, even in the darkest of times, a source of light will emerge to lead the way. This book is the perfect addition to any lunar lover's library!"

—Michael Herkes, author of *The GLAM Witch* and *The Complete Book of Moon Spells*, and contributor to *Witch Way* Magazine

"Magic is the way to manifest the life you want—but how does magic work? How do you manifest that magic? And that is why you have come to this wonderful book by Shaheen Miro. Reading this incredible magical work is to make a commitment to yourself to enter the shadows and walk among them to learn the correct way to harvest your own light and, like the moon, manifest that wonderful light on your life's path. *Lunar Alchemy* is a journey of exploration into the interior, a journey that will take you to meet your inner being, and, once there, embrace it with all the love that *both* of you (you and your inner yourself) deserve to receive."

—Elhoim Leafar, author of *The Magical Art of Crafting Charm Bags*

"Confidently, easily imbue yourself (and household objects) with power strong as the moon. This practical, comprehensive instruction guide blends inner work and magickal discipline. Illuminate your relationship to yourself, to the needs throughout your home and your everyday affairs. Honor eastern ideas and Jungian concepts and explore your alignment using Miro's visionary book."

—Tabitha Dial, author of *Creative Divination*

"*Lunar Alchemy* brings Shaheen's magical touch to an already magical subject, leaving the reader enthusiastically primed to work with the primal energies of the Moon. Delightfully weaving in both theory and practice, Shaheen brings fresh ideas and a gentle, motivating touch that is sure to enlighten newcomers and experienced practitioners alike!"

—Mantis, author of *Truly Easy Tarot*

"This is the moon magic book we have all been waiting for! With his typical blend of grace and charm, Shaheen guides us through the various ways we can work with the moon to create magic and alchemical transformation in our lives. The spells and enchantments are current, relevant, and potent. The perfect gift for any Lunar lover!"

—Briana Saussy, author of *Making Magic*

Lunar Alchemy

EVERYDAY MOON MAGIC
TO TRANSFORM
YOUR LIFE

SHAHEEN MIRO

WEISER
BOOKS

This edition published in 2020 by Weiser Books, an imprint of
Red Wheel/Weiser, LLC
With offices at
65 Parker Street, Suite 7
Newburyport, MA 01950
www.redwheelweiser.com

ISBN: 978-1-57863-690-7

Library of Congress Cataloging-in-Publication Data available upon request.

Typeset in Lato
Cover art and art page viii © Shaheen Miro

Printed in the United States of America
IBI
10 9 8 7 6 5 4 3 2 1

This book is dedicated to anyone
lost in the shadows . . . may you remember your light

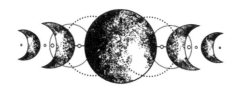

Contents

Living Your Magic

The moon is a constant in our lives. Every day, we experience the moon, and every day we have the opportunity to draw on moon magic to transform our lives. This book will introduce you to the four major moon phases—the Waning Moon, the New Moon, the Waxing Moon, and the Full Moon—and will provide you with exercises, meditations, rituals, ceremonies, and journaling prompts so that you may draw on the powerful transformative magic the moon has to offer. Phase by phase, you will learn to harness the magical energy of the moon as she passes through your life. However, this isn't simply a book about moon spells or moon magic. It is a book that ultimately will familiarize you with the phases of the moon as steps on the alchemical path—the Great Work—so that you can learn to internalize that alchemy as a tranformative force in your own life.

Wherever you are in life, you're experiencing a phase. Like the moon, you are on a journey from dark to light and back again. There are good days and bad days; days when you're filled with self-love and acceptance and off days when you're filled with self-loathing. How often do you bemoan, "What's wrong with me?" We put such high expectations on ourselves to be "perfect" all the time, and so we are in a constant state of accepting and rejecting ourselves. What a waste of the beautiful, natural magic that is you!

Your life's journey waxes and wanes like the moon. You are in a constant process from inward seeking to outward expression, a journey from introspection to manifest creation. Your life's path is, like the moon's, a series of phases—times of abundance, times of thin scarcity, times of light, times of darkness, times of feminine intuition, and times of masculine action. The cycle repeats. Like the moon, you change day to day. No one phase alone is "you"; no one phase is right, or better, or more moral than any other. You are the sum total of all your phases—and like the moon you are on a constant alchemical journey of change and transformation.

This book will help you embrace that change and use it to live your best life. Though life can feel daunting and you might feel stuck in a phase, *Lunar Alchemy* will show you that there's always magic to be discovered wherever you are, because the moon is always with you.

The moon has always been a traveler on the alchemical path. *Lunar Alchemy* is not just about the moon as an astronomical or astrological body; it is ultimately a book about the moon within you. *Lunar Alchemy* draws upon the energetic and metaphoric significance of the Moon and focuses on using the moon as a tool for self-awareness—as the key to creating change in your life. The moon is a metaphor for magic and transformation for all of us.

So what does this mean, the "moon within you"? Most books focus on what the moon is *doing*, but *Lunar Alchemy* takes an inward-out perspective, focusing what *you* are doing instead. In this book, I explore how we are all in a particular "phase" of our experience and, by using the moon as a guiding metaphor for that experience, we can gain deeper understanding of each particular personal phase and learn to work *with* it, rather than against it, to create fluid, magical momentum in life.

There is deep magic in the moon. But before you can internalize how the moon manifests within you, you must learn to journey with the moon throughout the year. *Lunar Alchemy* follows the path of the four major phases of the moon: the Waning Moon, the New Moon, the Waxing Moon, and the Full Moon. I will address each phase of the moon in part two of this book, and you will begin your journey by practicing the ceremonies and rituals during each of these major phases.

But does that mean you need to wait for a New Moon to address, say, rituals of creativity, potential, and new beginnings in your life—all New Moon issues? The answer is no. This book will teach you how to recognize the New Moon within you. It will teach you to dig deep into your innermost self to recognize and name your desires and intentions. This book is structured so that you may either work with New Moon energy during the actual New Moon phase or harness that energy when you recognize your inner New Moon rising.

You are the moon, and the moon is you. As above, so below. As within, so without.

In this book, you will work with oracles, ceremony, candle magic, exercises, and metaphor to understand your inner world. Throughout the lunar alchemy experience, you'll meet your Hungry Ghosts (the shadow) and your Shining Ones (the divine within). We will discuss the differences between the Lunar Self (feminine, creative, right-brained) and the Solar Self (masculine, logical, left-brained) and how that energy manifests in your world.

Lunar Alchemy will not focus on astrology, gender, or a specific religious/spiritual path. The process of the lunar alchemical experience begins with the waning and dark moon as a way to acquaint you with the shadow aspects of your self—the Hungry Ghosts. Beginning with this moon phase is essential because it's one thing to make a wish and set an intention, but it's a completely different thing to actually bring that intention to fruition. Successful manifesting begins with knowing where you are stuck or in resistance.

Most books on the moon focus specifically on the "wishing" aspect of the New Moon, and in my experience that is a limited approach because most people can name what they want, but aren't actually ready to receive it. So shadow work is a key element in the lunar alchemy experience, helping you align desire, intention, and action to create change.

In *Lunar Alchemy*, I use metaphor and language to bridge a gap for people between the inner and outer world and how the two go hand in hand for creating change and working magic.

Each exercise in *Lunar Alchemy* builds on the last, showing how the moon builds, expands, ebbs, flows, and goes through a cycle. This isn't a recipe-style book of spells, but a system and practice that will take you deeper and deeper into the introspection process so you can fully wield your innate creative power.

In *Lunar Alchemy* you will discover a new way of moving through the world. You'll learn to embrace the moon's progression through the sky, and as you do, something will be awakened, a strange stirring of magic that has always been within you. Let yourself be pulled by the moon in the ebb and flow with life; be like tides that move with graceful force.

• • •

Lunar Alchemy is presented in three parts. In part one, I discuss the alchemical concepts behind lunar magic: "as above, so below," how to work with energy and intuition, and the concept of manifestation through intention and perception.

Part two—the heart of the book—will present the four major phases of the moon and provide exercises and ceremonies for working with each phase both as it is manifested within in you and without you.

In part three I provide a selection of ceremonies and exercises geared toward specific intentions.

What I share here is my personal understanding of the moon and the ways in which she can enrich our lives. Move through these lessons with curiosity. Let yourself see through different eyes. Use what resonates with you and develop your own practices.

This book is a return to magic and a reminder that magic happens in every moment of every day. Simply going outside, peering up at the sky, and greeting the moon make up an initiation into the mysteries. With the moon as your guide, you are never alone; even when her light doesn't shine, she is there.

Each phase of the moon is an invitation for you to participate in your life experience and draw upon the magic that is natural and intrinsic to you. *Lunar Alchemy* is a magical, holistic approach to life. By aligning yourself with the moon, you willl come to learn your own ebb and flow of energy and power. You will discover that your inner world creates your outer experience—the alchemical maxim of "as above, so below." With this understanding, you will begin to see that all things in life are interconnected—if one thing is lacking, then everything suffers.

The practices in this book are geared toward anyone interested in magic for introspection, radical self-care, and personal empowerment. Magic is an innate force within you. I want us all to venerate our deeper connection to nature, to the invisible forces outside of our immediate awareness.

We then become the alchemical masters of our own lives.

PART ONE

Preparing for
Your Lunar Journey

CHAPTER 1

The Moon Is Your Mirror

Imagine a velvety black sky above you, encrusted with diamond stars. Night after night you notice a sliver of light growing in the sky. Where there was nothing, a crescent has formed. Each passing night, the crescent of light grows larger, rounder, and fuller—growing until the whole night sky is lit with a silver mirror cascading light over shadows and pulling the tides.

The moon is a powerful metaphor of transformation and growth. She shows us how to embody our own energetic evolution and step into our magic. Lunar alchemy engages the inner oracle—your wisest self that speaks the language of metaphor and knows beyond words or explanation. What the moon will teach you will challenge your intellect and awaken your Lunar Self.

Since ancient times, people have felt called to the moon. Some would track time by her light, knowing that her cycle lasted for 29.5 days. With keen intuitive knowing and observation they witnessed her influence over nature: the growth of crops, the behavior of animals, the fecundity of menstruation, and the pull of the tides.

And as we are part of the web of nature, the moon exerts her profound influence over us. She literally pulls our internal tides.

Each step you take during your exploration of the moon is an invitation to discover your own magic. The moon reflects you, you reflect the moon. There is no separation. Go forward with subtle perception. You can't think your way through the moonlight; you have to feel yourself forward.

A key component of moon magic, and all natural magic, is intuition and feeling. There is a time and place for logic—that part of us that is ruled by the sun—and just as the sun and moon are in right-relationship with one another, our logic and intuition are also two sides of the same coin. *Lunar Alchemy* is a return to the Lunar Self, the part of you that dreams, feels, imagines, and stirs. You will learn the language of the moon by always asking: how do I feel?

Practice checking in with yourself on a daily basis to enhance this shift in perspective. Simply close your eyes and ask: How do I feel right now? You'll be surprised at how clarifying this question can be. So much is happening under the surface, subconsciously brewing in your heart and being left unacknowledged.

Take this practice a step further and begin feeling the moon. Notice how you feel during each phase of the moon. Different phases affect us in different ways. Are you anxious? What phase is the moon in? Are you in love? What phase is the moon in now? Learn to correlate the "moon within" with the "moon without." When you move with the ebb and flow of the moon, your own energy becomes more powerful. Eventually you will feel the moon phase without having to peer at the sky.

The lunar alchemical experience revolves around the four major phases of the moon.

The Waning Moon

Alchemical phase: Nigredo

We begin our journey when the moon's light begins to fade into blackness. Energetically the Waning Moon is a time of release and surrender. We are drawn inward for stillness, reflection, and recalibration. This is a time of parting with the old, so you can stretch into the new.

The New Moon

Alchemical phase: Albedo

The second phase we will work with is the New Moon when her light is nothing more than a silver crescent in the sky. The New Moon is raw potential. This is a time to sow seeds of intention, to influence positive growth.

The Waxing Moon

Alchemical phase: Citrinitas

The third phase in the moon's progression is waxing when her face is equally light and dark. As the moon gains light and increases in size, her energy lends to focus, clarification, and an increase in your desires.

The Full Moon

Alchemical phase: Rubedo

This is the fourth phase, when the face of the moon is fully illuminated. As a bright lantern in the sky, she shows the proof—the outcome—of your intentional work. This is a time of fulfillment, celebration, and reaffirmation. I think of the Full Moon as a threshold—you've arrived at this moment only to embark on another journey of increase . . . the next lunation.

• • •

Nature works in a constant cycle of creation. Death becomes the doorway to life and life moves into death again. When the moon goes dark, we know she will find her light again. You are like the moon, constantly going through a process of growing, revealing, and retreating into stillness. The possibility is always there.

Sometimes you'll find yourself stuck in a phase, usually the dark phase where everything feels cloudy, confusing, and disjointed. When you're stifled by something, life is cumbersome, precarious, painful, and blocked. You *know* that feeling—in some way you sense your full power is obscured by the shadows of your life. But a deep pull inside of you beckons you forward, encouraging you to increase your light until you bloom into full expression.

We will follow the light of the moon and engage with her powerful energies of change. By tapping into the moon's energetic framework, you can move back into the flow, the natural law of increased life—day by day you move into your process of becoming. This is how your life begins to thrive.

CHAPTER 2

As Above, So Below

Life is strange, interesting, and beautiful. We live in a time of great change—the paradigm is shifting, the dominant power is tipping in a new direction. We're seeing, experiencing, and witnessing many heavy, abrasive, and completely shocking things from within our own psyche, the people around us, and the planet as a whole.

Regardless of your place in life, you've seen how fragmented our world is becoming. No one is immune to the struggles we're all facing. But although I write this in 2020, our world has, in fact, been under the seductive influence of power and manipulation for longer than any of us have been around. From one generation to the next, we've been conditioned to feel, think, and believe that we are all pawns in this game called life.

Society has functioned on a precarious foundation of power and domination—over others, over money and resources, over our own sovereignty. In an aim to dominate whatever is perceived as "less than," cycles of pain, fear, and destruction are perpetuated.

My personal view is that this drive toward domination is a mutation of our Solar/masculine self. The Solar Self is the part of us that seeks to take action, to do, to build, to control. When this part of us becomes imbalanced or unconscious, it seeks to dominate. And, this is the source of grasping, greed, and selfishness we see in the world right now.

But the power is shifting. We are going through a cosmic evolution. The collective consciousness is evolving into to something different, tipping to the other side of the spectrum, to hopefully create equilibrium. We are experiencing a shift to the Lunar Self, which seeks power from within. We are rediscovering how to be empowered by our own receptive, intuitive nature.

When we begin to honor the power within, we begin to have empathy, compassion, and respect for each other. Because there is no longer a need to dominate or control, we see the interconnectedness of all life. If I thrive, you thrive. If we are well, the planet is well.

As above, so below.

Power within doesn't seek to take, destroy, or dominate because it has no sense of competition. Within each of us is a cornucopia of blessings; your divine supply is ever abundant; you just need to open the door and awaken the connection.

As the embodiment of feminine energy, the moon teaches us how to align with our creative, nurturing aspects. Our inner truth is revealed through lunar light. By crossing the threshold into the inner chambers of your soul, you'll discover how to heal the disconnection between your Lunar and Solar Selves.

Nothing is lost in this alchemical process of unification; all aspects of your consciousness are integrated as a whole. It is in this metamorphosis through which your inner wisdom breaks free to guide and direct your path and purpose.

So what does this mean for you?

You've picked up this book, so you're a rebel of sorts. You have made the brave commitment to step into the shadows and cultivate your light. Through the ups and downs of life, you've discovered that there must be more than just struggling to get by and ambling through uncertainty. You feel the undercurrent of your personal power and magic coursing through your core, begging to break free into expression.

That inkling is the first step into personal empowerment. You've discovered you have a choice—to either let life happen *to* you or create a life that is working *for* you. Embracing that feeling of personal empowerment is the key to your transformation.

Look around you! People want to be seen and heard for who and what they are. No longer will the Lunar Self stay quiet. She is seeking expression, and pushing through every fracture of our psyche to break free.

Old habits are hard to break; we cling to what we know regardless of how much it hurts. There's safety in the familiar. Change is a natural part of life, and we must embrace the new wave or get tumbled about in the current.

Stepping onto this radical path of change is a challenge. You're facing your fears, listening to your pain, and destroying all the old learning that has perpetuated for millennia. This means you have to stand up for yourself. Be willing to challenge what you know, let go of your limiting beliefs, and stretch yourself in ways you never have before.

I know you are capable of it because you have desire. And our desires are the soul's way of expressing possibility. Whatever you desire on a deep level can be made real because it lives in your vibration. If it weren't a possibility, you wouldn't have the desire.

Wanting something deeply is proof of the possibility. Remember this as we move deeper into the lunar experience.

So you've prayed for change. You've heard the call. You've listened. Now is your chance to step into your magic, empower yourself, and begin to express your unique purpose out in the world. Moving forward you must be brave, curious, and willing to observe the life around you . . . without judgment.

It begins with choice.

Inner transformation happens with a choice. Choose to do things differently. Choose to live differently. Choose to take action differently. Choose to move through experiences differently.

Maybe you didn't always know you had a choice?

Many of us were raised in environments that robbed us of personal choice. Since childhood you've been taught how to be, who to be, what to be. You were told how to show up and what to do. You've inherited a set of beliefs from a long line of unconscious living. Mostly, these beliefs were pressed upon you with good intention, to keep you safe and help you survive life.

To put it simply, we've all been conditioned, and the conditioning is on repeat . . . for you, for me, for society.

But we can disrupt the cycle. We can actually choose what we want to believe, who we want to be, and how we show up in the world. Think about the beliefs you've inherited. Do they make you feel good? Do you ever question them? Can you see how these beliefs have shaped your life?

Look at how convincing and insidious these inherited beliefs have been. They have perpetuated fears, manifested traumas, and created chronic cycles in your life, and the lives of those before you. I know if you look at your family's collective history, you can see the cycles of pain time and time again. And the truth is, everyone is doing their best with what they have and what they know.

You have a chance to choose something different. With a new perspective you can move forward. Making this choice allows you to overcome your conditioning, to heal your trauma, to be bigger than your problems. Choice allows us to disrupt the cycle and, in a sense, collectively heal the pain of our lineage.

Lunar Alchemy works under an ancient principle that states: "As above, so below. As within, so without."

To truly understand this statement you must know that you are a divine being, a creative force in the Universe. You are not separate from the divine (in whatever form you wish to see it), but an extension of the divine.

Or understand it this way: You are a part of nature; just as a tree has a natural cycle, so do you. Both you and the tree are always in the process of increasing your life, expressing your unique, divine purpose, and creating for creation's sake.

The tree doesn't question that it is a tree, meant to grow roots and limbs to touch the sky. But you and I, humans, we do question what we are here for. We run on an inner dialogue that tells us one way to be (learned from the outside voices of conditioning) and yet a feeling inside desires to be another way (the intrinsic knowing).

As above, so below expresses the truth that all of nature is meant to flow, cycle, express, and create. It is divine law, right, and purpose. You're meant to thrive in life, rather than endure it. Your soul is always in need of growth, expression, and creation. If you halt this process, then you halt life.

As within, so without.

What does stifled life look like?

When you are no longer living from your soul center, your inner wisdom, your internal state becomes fragmented. That inner state manifests outward as the state of your life. What you feel inside becomes the way your life looks on the outside. Whatever experience you are having out here in the world is being mirrored from your inner world because life is holographic: you are literally projecting outward into the world the movie of your inner world, whether you are conscious of doing so or not.

The moon is a mirror. She represents the self and what is behind the self. Her power and energy can show us how to go within to heal the wounds and mend the cracks, which in turn will change our life experience.

In *Lunar Alchemy*, we will explore different ways of entering the lunar side—our inner landscape. Crossing that threshold allows you to see the fragments and shadows as they are, without judgment, so you can truly understand them and move past them.

This work is alchemy. Alchemy is the process of transmuting one form into another. In ancient time, alchemy was the process of turning base metal into gold and ultimately discovering the philosophers' stone. You will begin to transmute your own tarnished parts into gold and ultimately discover the power within that grants you wisdom and purpose eternal.

Manifestation

Life is happening *for* you, rather than *to* you. What does that actually mean?

What you experience in physical reality is directly connected to what you're experiencing on an internal level. The experience is a manifestation of a vibration. You've created the experience based on a deeply held belief pattern that has led to thoughts, actions, emotions—these in turn create, attract, and crystallize those beliefs.

Let me step back and say that this isn't a statement meant to induce guilt, shame, or blame. In fact, this should be a freeing statement, something that lets you know the immense power you have in this life. And before your rational mind gets the better of you, know that you will never "figure" it all out . . .

By knowing that everything is an "outing" of your inner world, you get to be more curious about life. You get to partake in the dance and find your rhythm through the experience. Endeavor to taste the raw, juicy nature of life. And slip back into the knowing that you are here to express yourself.

Most of us look at life in terms of duality.

We categorize experiences as good or bad. We want fewer bad experiences and more good ones. We want more light and less shadow. But shadow is the thing that cradles the light. The "contrast," as you might call it, allows you to see where you can move, change, and transform more.

Much of what you believe to be true isn't based on your own experience; it was impressed upon you early on. Up to this point, you've spent a whole life proving those beliefs, experience after experience. Through *Lunar Alchemy*, you will learn to disrupt the program, open your awareness, and ask questions.

Asking questions, knowing you have a choice, is what allows magic to manifest in your life.

Do you remember as a child coloring, drawing, or painting? There were no hard lines, no parameters. You could literally play in whatever way you desired. A dog could have wings. People could be magical. Pets could talk. Trees could give hugs. A scribble on a page could tell a whole story.

Give a child three crayons and they can paint a whole picture. Give an adult three crayons and they will probably ask for the only color not there. If you allow yourself to see the possibility, rather than the limitation, you become empowered.

Nothing in your life is happening to punish you. Everything is happening to open you up, to expand your awareness, to encourage your growth. Take creative leaps!

Notice . . . notice everything.
How can you play in this moment with exactly what you have?
How can you create something from nothing?
How can you spin straw into gold?

How can you turn lead into the Philosophers' Stone?

What will you do with your magic?

If you see life as your canvas and your experiences as inspiration, who knows what you can dream up and make real? Yes, there will be those moments where you feel completely overwhelmed by life. Something will happen that convinces you that life is actually happening to you. And you'll feel like there's nothing you can do about it. You will feel stuck in a phase.

When you are stuck in a phase, your inner life has become oppositional: your rational mind craves one thing, and your inner knowing desires something completely different.

Through the exercises in *Lunar Alchemy*, you will learn to become aware of this experience—the manifestation of the internal conflict. It is literally being revealed to you so you can see the disparity. Once you recognize it, then you can work your light to be more deliberate, to be congruent, to become whole.

As within, so without.

What is happening in your outer world is a reflection of your inner state. *The moon is your mirror.* Becoming aware of this feedback allows you to move deeper into the uncovering, the revealing, and the choosing.

In the next chapter, we will introduce the first lunar exercise: naming and claiming the phase you are in.

CHAPTER 3

Your Energetic Story

Everything in the Universe is energy. What you see, feel, and experience is the manifestation of an energetic vibration. Energy is the invisible thread that ties everything together. It knows no space or time.

We are exploring the world of energy—specifically, your energetic story. Your energetic story is the accumulation of your thoughts, ideas, beliefs, fears, and feelings about life and how life responds to you. Your energetic story becomes the narrative of your life. As we work with the moon, your energetic story will be revealed, and you can begin shifting this energy in conscious and powerful ways.

The foundation of your inner world is laid by your experiences; over time those experiences become your beliefs. In every moment we look for proof of what we believe, whether those beliefs are good or bad, nourishing or depleting, conscious or unconscious.

Your inner world becomes your outer reality. Reality is relative to the inner experience, which is continuously looping, unless you disrupt the cycle with conscious attention. If you couple attention with clear intention and follow those intentions with action, then action and ownership create empowered change.

When you tap into your energetic story, you begin to see the narrative of your life. That narrative can be changed to reflect a more congruent and coherent version of you! You make conscious the unconscious parts of you and shine light into the dark and forgotten places of your inner world.

Remember, you get to choose what you believe. And by making the choice with deliberate intention and action, you claim ownership of your life; you change the vibration, and that manifests outward in your life experience.

To put it simply, your energetic story is your point of attraction.

If every thought or feeling holds a vibration, and that vibration is something you immerse yourself in regularly, then it becomes your state of being. That frequency or vibration is what you broadcast out into the Universe, pushing and pulling equal vibrations into your experience. The more time we spend in any one vibrational state, the denser the energy becomes until it manifests in physical reality.

So one negative thought doesn't create a negative life. But a repeated negative thought becomes a negative belief, and that negative belief becomes your vibrational state, which means you can and will only create a reality that supports your vibration.

Can you name an experience in your life where this has been true?

You might not know the roots of your pain, but you can usually name the discomfort you're experiencing. So we begin our process in the here and now, looking at the state of your life: Your pain and fears.

Your desires and celebrations. Rather than seeing them as something separate from you or out of your control, you'll begin to see the silver thread that connects everything in your experience together.

Your thoughts, your feelings, and your actions have been and always are the generative force behind your life. To apply the alchemical experience of the moon will mean tapping into your thoughts and feelings in an open and honest way and using them as a ladder to climb deeper inside to find the source of your pain and power, all with the moon as a guide.

The First Exercise: What Phase Are You In?

Begin by making two lists:

1. A list of the things that you feel dim your light and rob you of energy/confidence/power/authority.

2. A list of the things that feed you're your light and increase your energy.

Now ask yourself the following questions to see what phase you are in. The answers to these questions will clue you in on how you are using your energy and what stage of development your personal power, desires, and intentions seem to be in.

Sometimes you'll find a specific area of your life is in one phase. Generally there is an overall energetic state in which we spend most of our time.

A Waning Moon Phase:

Are you tired, lethargic or drained?

Are situations coming to a close?

Are certain people leaving your life?

Do you feel blocked or facing hurdles?

Do you lack new ideas or feel unimaginative?

Are you sleeping more?

Does talking, exercising, or high-energy activities feel hard?

Are you craving "heavy" foods?

Do you feel the need to withdraw?

Do you feel like receiving?

Do you feel depressed or antisocial?

Often, when we are energetically in a Waning Moon phase, things are winding down and coming to a close. This means there is a need to hibernate, go inward, and rest. Action isn't necessary at this time; being is the good medicine. Eating grounding foods and restful practices will help you move with this energy, rather than against it.

A New Moon Phase:

Are you experiencing a flood of ideas?

Do you feel like you've just woken up?

Are you jittery?

Do you feel like something is "coming" but don't know what?

Are you meeting new people or getting new offers?

Do you feel called to start something?

Have you been more active?

Do you want to do something, but don't know how or what?

Do you feel thirsty or crave more water?

Do you want to plan things out?

Do you feel unbridled?

Being in New Moon phase can feel like the start of something. You might lack specific direction, but the energy is there. It feels like waking up from a power nap and wanting to dive in. You might have to wipe the sleep from your eyes, but desire for action is there. When you are in this phase, drinking water or taking a bath can feel nourishing, and it helps your psychic receptors work more fluidly. A great way to move with this energy is trying some new form of exercise or doing something that gets your mind going—games, puzzles, and so on. And doing a mind-dump of ideas can help you get out of your head and start seeing what steps will come next.

A Waxing Moon Phase:

Do you feel more certain about yourself or your goals?

Do you have a clear picture?

Are you more perceptive to people or situations?

Do you get a "yes" or "no" feeling about things?

Are you decisive?

Are you eating more?

Do you have high energy or feel buoyant?

Are things lining up or falling into place?

Have you experienced a series of unexpected synchronicities?

Are people reaching out to you?

Do you feel like giving?

Do you feel magnetic or attractive?

The Waxing Moon phase is where energy builds. You will feel more "on point" and ready to take action in clear ways. Making simple decisions quickly will help you move with this energy. For example, you could give yourself thirty seconds to decide which drink you want at your local café or what outfit you will wear for the day. Making a list of actions steps for the day or week will feel good. You might feel hungrier because of the high energy that is moving through you. Because your energy is ramping up, you'll find opportunities show up with ease, people are reaching out to you, and synchronicities are more common. You're very magnetic.

A Full Moon Phase:

Do you feel bold?

Do you feel shining?

Are you feeling full, bloated, or overeating?

Are you feeling intense or overtalkative?

Are you fixated on something?

Do you feel like you've gotten too deep into your goal?

Do you want to change, but feel like you can't go back?

Are you overwhelmed?

Have you completed something major?

Do you see an end in sight?

Are you facing a threshold?

Are you giving "birth" to something?

Are you creating at light speed?

A Full Moon phase feels like big, bold energy. Usually, this is a time when you feel larger than life—for better or worse. You're in the thick of whatever you are doing or creating. Sometimes you'll feel like you are too far in to turn back. You might find your energy being a bit electric; you're supercharged . . . which could make you extra chatty, restless, or even scattered because so much is happening. When you're in this phase, you're about to cross a threshold. Think about it like giving birth. You've put a lot into something, and now a new chapter needs to begin.

Journaling the Lunar Journey

Begin your notebook by naming and claiming your phase: write down the answers to the above questions and note which moon phase they indicate. Note whether your energy seems more inclined to one phase or another. Make this exercise a daily journal entry, and see if you can start to notice patterns and cycles of your energy.

Cycles, Phases, and Transformation

Life works in cycles. We move through phases of expression, evolution, and embodiment. Who you are at the beginning of this experience isn't who you will become as you transform yourself. You will shed layers, let down veils, and reveal the brighter side of yourself. Waking up to something bigger than before, you will never go back to sleep—you might grow drowsy, you might need retreat, but you will never forget the feeling of working your light.

Let the moon guide you. Her power is always present when you need it. But the moon is only a mirror; she reminds you that you're always powerful. You're always filled with light. You can choose to shine and express yourself in whatever way you like.

If you leave with anything, let it be this: life isn't happening to you, it is happening *for* you, *because* of you. Even when you forget your place as divine creator, you're still creating. There is no way to turn it off, to shut it down, to keep it at bay.

Set this clear intention as you work with the moon: *"I am the deliberate creator of my life."*

Intention and Perception

Exploring your potential coupled with the power of the moon begins by shifting your perception of yourself, life, and reality. Imagination is the gateway to this alternate perception. If you try to understand your lunar adventure by rationalizing the experience through your solar eyes, you will limit the immense power that is available to you.

Leave fear, doubt, worry, and judgment at the door. Get ready for your adventure playing in the moonlight. Let yourself be curious.

Throughout this book, you will increase your intuitive fluency by working with oracles, ritual, inner visioning, and metaphor. Each of these tools offers another lens to peek through and understand the breadth and depth of your personal power and potential. I see each of these tools as a way to unify the connection between your inner and outer world in an effort to be in right-relationship or agreement on all levels.

Metaphor in particular is the thread that pulls the whole process together. Intuition uses the language of metaphor to express profound insights by giving them a shape and form that regular language and logic cannot. Working with metaphor in this way expands your perception and understanding of events, situations, and experiences.

Over time, you will find this new understanding allows you to actually work through cycles and situations in your life so you can heal, evolve, and expand yourself in ways you couldn't imagine before.

In part two of this book, you will meet your Hungry Ghosts and your Shining Ones. You might find yourself asking, are these beings real, with a life and intelligence of their own? Or are they are just figments of your imagination?

The answer to both questions is yes. Try not to get stuck on this concept by thinking about them logically. Remember to look through the eyes of metaphor. Whether or not you see them as real, living entities or facets of yourself doesn't matter because they are all expressions of energy. Through imagination you can communicate with these energies in a very real and tangible way.

There is metaphysical concept called a Tulpa. A Tulpa is a thought-form that has been charged and imbued with so much energy and intention that it takes on a life and intelligence of its own. Some magical practitioners consciously create a Tulpa as an ally to help them see, hear, know, or accomplish certain tasks. Though the Tulpa is birthed from the consciousness of the creator, it has a very real life of its own.

You could think of the Hungry Ghosts and Shining Ones in much the same way—they are extensions of you birthed through your thoughts, feelings, and experiences. However, their creation happens on a sub-conscious or unintended level. Once you rekindle your connection with these energies—with conscious intention—you can work with them to learn, understand, and accomplish so many things.

Or simply think of it like this: When you externalize some aspect of yourself, you gain a different way of interacting with that aspect. You can see and understand it with expanded awareness. It's almost like looking at something from a bird's-eye view.

Magic is paradoxical.

What I want to express to you is this: In the effort to understand yourself more, you have to be okay with the mystery of things. Lunar alchemy isn't about figuring anything out, it's about discovering how to move more fully into expression.

Lets consider the process of dreaming . . .

Lucid Dreaming

As you sleep, your mind is filled with fantastic stories that could offer some deeper truth. You're open and receptive to the whispers of your soul. It is said that dreams are really a mirror of your subconscious mind, and your subconscious mind is your Lunar Self. Some would even say that every character in a dream represents some facet of the dreamer. Your Lunar Self speaks in metaphors, offering symbolic stories to help express a deeper personal gnosis.

According to Jeffrey Sumber, "Dreams are the bridge that allows movement back and forth between what we think we know and what we really know."* These inner narratives act as a bridge between the conscious mind and the subconscious mind, a way of revealing the powerful stories that are at work in every aspect of waking life.

Often when you wake in the morning, these dreams become nothing but fragments, foggy impressions of some peculiar events that seem to have no roots in reality. And yet they seem so alluring; when a fragment reemerges in the waking hours, summoned by some connecting force, it leaves us wondering more.

---

* From an interview with Jeffrey Sumber at *psychcentral.com*.

These impressions are typically fleeting because we wake up and move back into "rational reality," the Solar Self. We either dismiss the dream altogether or we see it as gibberish, because the Solar Self has no understanding of the symbolic nature of the Lunar. You have to look through the right eyes to truly understand these impressions.

We want to rationalize our dreams because we want to do something with them. But doing is not being. The deeper you go into lunar alchemy, the more you are called into being. "Being" means that you are present, in the here and now, to see, feel, and experience whatever is happening around you, to you, for you—because of you.

The more you allow yourself to be present—because the present moment is where the power lies—the more real your life becomes, until you finally discover that you are in a waking dream!

Journaling the Lunar Journey

Lucid dreaming is one way to set your intention and become more conscious of your Lunar Self. Lucid dreaming simply means that you are in a conscious state during your dreaming, and it's a technique that can be learned. There are several good books available to help you hone this ability. For the purposes of the lunar alchemy experience, I highly recommend that you keep a dream journal or dream diary, as a way to capture your powerful inner stories. Make a note of the moon phase during your dream—this information will provide additional insight that you can come back to later.

The Truth about Oracles

Oracles are the utterances of your soul. The word *oracle* literally means "speak" or "expressed by divine inspiration." When you experience an oracle in any form, you are hearing/experiencing an expression of your soul. Oracles are manifestations of inner wisdom. When you receive an oracle message, you are getting confirmation of something you know on a very deep level.

There are many tools that are oracular: oracle decks, Lenormand Cards, the Tarot, pendulums, palmistry, crystals, to name a few. I personally work most often with the Tarot and with oracle decks—I encourage you, for the purposes of lunar work, to try the *Lunar Nomad Oracle* which I designed specifically to teach and enhance the lunar journey.

Oracle messages are not premonitions of what *could* be; they are the voice of what already *is* on a vibrational level. Messages received through an oracle are both confirmation of what you already know and a call for you to pay attention—a way of choosing to go deeper into that experience or change vibration to create something new.

See the oracle as the seed. You know it holds a possibility deep inside, something that is already stirring to life. If you plant it, water it, nurture it—it will grow. Are you growing light or feeding shadows? Are you cultivating a garden or leaving it to weeds?

Oracles are a language, a way of having a conversation with your inner world. When you see oracles as another means for feedback, you understand their full power as a tool for making choices.

When I read for someone, I always describe it as revealing that person's energetic story.

You get to write the narrative. The future is fluid; time is fluid—you are always creating based on your inner state. To read a fortune is to read the level of awareness and quality of choice someone is making. You're locked into fate only to the degree to which you choose to be unconscious—you get to make a choice!

You could think of it this way: you can read the story or you can write the story. So see your oracle messages as a way of choosing. The oracle is revealing to you your own energetic story.

If you receive an oracular message that doesn't make sense, let go of the need to understand, and allow yourself to just feel. Sometimes the information needs time to settle in; often we look at a reading through the Solar Self—trying to intellectually understand it—like interpreting a dream, rather than feeling it through the Lunar Self where the knowing just aligns.

When you're ready for a message and fully receptive, it truly feels like confirmation. When a message hits you and feels lopsided or doesn't resonate, it isn't that the message is wrong—you're just not ready to receive it. It is another way of cracking you open, allowing you to observe and follow the path inward.

See there's no way to get this wrong. The only line in the sand is the one you draw with your mind.

Journaling the Lunar Journey

As you make use of oracles in the lunar alchemical process, write down the messages you receive. In particular, when you get a message or experience you don't want, ask yourself:

What part of me wants this to be true?

What part of me is fighting the truth?

Why does it feel good, bad, right, or wrong?

How is it serving me?

How am I embodying this message now?

What would I like to embody instead?

Remember that the message isn't good or bad. It either challenges or confirms your present alignment—not just the thoughts in your head, but the feelings and beliefs swirling around below.

PART TWO

The Phases
of the Moon

CHAPTER 5

Working Phase by Phase

We will move through each phase of the moon, beginning with the Waning Moon. Beginning with this phase may seem odd to some people familiar with moon magic because it is a time of ending, release, and parting. In my personal practice, I have found this is the best phase to begin with because it allows you to cultivate the fertile space to plant and nourish new desires.

In each chapter that follows, I will share the energetic invitation of the moon; alchemical concepts relating to this phase; exercises, meditations, and ceremonies to work with her potential; as well as lunar correspondences and journaling prompts. I encourage you to move through each chapter along with the astronomical moon phase so you can get the most benefit from your work. You might want to read through once before beginning your practice in real time.

My intention is to teach you a practical way to work with each phase. You will begin by working in a general way and get more specific with your desires as you go deeper with each phase. Think of this process as releasing, making space, honing in on an intention, growing feeling, and reaping the results. And then it all begins again with a new lunar cycle.

Working with the moon is an exciting process because it never ends. Cycles continue on and on into infinity. So with each phase and each practice you are going deeper, uncovering new layers of healing and potential. Eventually you will find specific intentions to take to the moon and work through them over a lunation or lunar cycle—some may last more than one lunation or be an ongoing endeavor.

Acquaint yourself with the moon by spending time noticing how your personal energy is ebbing and flowing, waxing and waning. Because working with the moon is about learning to be perceptive to subtle shifts and changes in energy, you should make a habit of seeing the moon in real time. Be sure to go outside often to see what the moon looks like. You can identify the phase by the shape, light, and orientation of the moon's placement in the sky. Then you can use a resource like *TimeandDate.com* to see what the current moon phase is.

For each moon practice, you will need specific tools and ingredients. Most of these are simple household items that you will already have on hand. I encourage you to plan ahead and gather anything you might need. You will also need a deck of oracle cards, such as the *Lunar Nomad Oracle*, and a journal.

Preparing for Your Moon Voyage

Are you ready for your moon voyage?

Everything in *Lunar Alchemy* is meant to cultivate space and aware-ness that will encourage your personal transformation. This is a holistic approach to life-changing magic. As you hold the space for yourself to transform, your perspective of life will gradually change, and eventually your whole life will change along with it.

Each practice you learn in each moon phase will be a tool for accomplishing this shift. In this section, I want to share some foundational work that will support all you endeavor to do with this book.

Magic Begins with Stillness

The world is fast-paced. High-energy environments overwhelm our senses and halt the connection to our deeper self. Without this connection, everything becomes stifled and chaotic. You can see this in the drama on the news, the depression that permeates our society, and the lack of openness we experience in daily life.

Working with the moon will rekindle this connection. This is a practice; you must be dedicated to your transformation in order to see results. A fleeting dance with the moon will do little to bring about substantial and sustainable changes. Begin your practice by making time for stillness.

Most of us spend our time immersed in the gravity of daily life and responsibility, which pulls us away from our inner connection. You need a cocoon to spend time away from those demands where you can be still and consciously connect with your magic.

Being still doesn't mean physically standing in one place. It means opening up to become aware, more perceptive of your inner self.

Stillness—as in meditation, prayer, or simple silence—signals to your awareness that you're crossing the threshold from the mundane to the mystical. Here you can contemplate the invitation of each moon phase and perform ceremonies and practices to feel, touch, and experience these energies in a very visceral way.

It is in these moments you step outside of time. You can surrender to your inner wisdom and know that you need, want, and deserve to fulfill your highest good. In time you will discover how validating it is to take time for yourself. The more you care for yourself, the more light you can shine on other people around you.

Stillness allows you to become more perceptive to your own ebb and flow of energy. Sometimes the simplest thing you can do when you are in need of change is to stop, get still, and listen to what your body is saying. Then you can pinpoint thoughts, emotions, and patterns that are present and get clearer on what practical actions you are or are not taking right now.

Your whole moon voyage should begin with intentional time to be still. You are creating sacred moments and sacred space in your life so you can hear and distinguish between the voice of your inner wisdom and the voice of limiting beliefs running through your consciousness. You can never truly hear all the beautiful things your spirit is trying to tell you until you stop and listen!

STILLNESS EXERCISE

- Take a moment to close your eyes. Focus on your breathing. Find a rhythm with your breath as you inhale and exhale. Imagine each breath like the ebb and flow of the ocean—in and out, back and forth, rising and falling.

- Sense the earth beneath you, supporting you with ease. Sense the sky above you, drawing you upward and expanding your awareness. Feel how easy it is to be in this moment. Just surrender.

- Now turn your attention inward. Notice your present state of mind. Notice the thoughts passing through your mind. Notice feelings moving through your heart. Notice the sensations moving through your body.

- Become keenly aware of whatever is happening within you. And ask these questions:

  What does it look like inside?
  What does it feel like?
  What word would I use to describe this moment right now?

It's okay if this practice overwhelms you at first. Most of us are intimidated by going inward. It can feel rough, facing all the stuff going on inside. But you're a brave seeker and your journey starts by going inward.

Stillness Practices

Each of these methods will enhance your inner awareness and sense of stillness.

Meditation: Spend a few minutes daily in meditation. This can be done before you begin your day or just when you end it. You don't have to do a formal meditation. Just sitting with your eyes closed, noticing your breath, and letting yourself *be* for ten minutes a day will yield powerful results.

Prayer: Prayer is often us asking for guidance, but the heart of prayer—the real secret—is to stop and listen. What feelings do you get? What vibration is firing through you as you are communicating with the divine?

Movement: Connecting with your body cultivates a stillness that leads to self-insight. Move with awareness, using your body as a link between mind and spirit. I find the places where I hold tension give clues to where/how I am being rigid with life. Yoga is one of my favorite ways to facilitate this experience. In a yoga pose, I know immediately whether I am connected to my body and breath. Any movement practice will work, such as, a long walk, exercise, stretching, or self-massage. Notice your body. If the pain or sensation you feel were a metaphor, what would it mean? For example: If your upper back and neck hurt, you might contemplate the question: "What weight am I carrying on my shoulders? How can I put it down?"

Tea: Enjoy a warm cup of tea. Let yourself smell all the lovely aromas and feel the steam open up your head. Take a sip and swirl the liquid around your tongue. Actually *taste* the tea (or whatever you're drinking). This will allow you to be present, to observe whatever is happening in that moment. And it's *so* soothing!

Bathe: Take a nice long bath and let the tension of your day melt from your body. Don't rush or worry. You are in this moment relaxing. Let the steam and the bubbles and all the delicious scents clear your head and heart. Sing and smile and close your eyes. Some of the best revelations come in a warm bath.

Animals: Spend more time with your pets. These spirit babies are gifts from the Universe, sent here to add unconditional love and understanding to your life. They help to transmute negative energy and turn it into positive and productive energy. When you connect with the pure feelings of love, you link into your intuitive self.

Music: Take time to listen to good, uplifting music. Let the words and sounds enter you. Sing along or just close your eyes and drift away. Music isn't meant to be background noise. It's meant to be a doorway to another world where you can feel and experience something inside of you or something more expansive than you. Open up and let go for a while.

• • •

As you move through the levels of stillness, you are creating internal sacred space. Giving yourself this space allows you to tap into all of your wisdom. This is really the heart of spirituality.

Creating Sacred Space

Humans have been erecting sacred spaces since the beginning of time. Every spiritual tradition has its sacred places and holy sites. Some of them are so old that we know little about their significance, yet their sacred energy still permeates the area. Many natural places hold a mystical quality that has no connection to time or tradition; some people even believe these are key energy centers of the earth.

Sacred space is both a physical place and an internal state. Anywhere can be sacred with intention. Build your own place of power where you can safely dream, explore, and transform yourself. This should be somewhere that encourages your practice.

Wherever you choose to create sacred space, you will need an altar. An altar is nothing more than a special surface dedicated to housing power items and performing ceremony.

A side table, shelf, or bookcase is a wonderful surface for an altar. I personally like to use a silver tray for my moon altar so that I can easily change locations—to a window so I can see the moon, to the bathroom so I can perform a cleansing bath, or to the outdoors.

Choose your altar and a place where you'd like to create sacred space for the time being. Choose a surface with enough room to house the curios you will collect throughout your practice. Wherever you choose to erect your altar, make sure it's comfortable to sit in front of for long periods of time. This will be the focal point of your moon voyage.

Prepare Your Sacred Space

Now you can begin preparing your sacred space for your spiritual work. Wash the surface of your altar with warm water. As you do this imagine everything being filled with positive energy. You are washing away the physical dirt and the energetic debris that might be attached to the object. Be sure to wash anything you add to your altar if possible. If you can't wash it with water, then just imagine it being filled with high vibration.

You can cover your altar with a tablecloth or special scarf. A piece of white silk or cotton is a great choice. If you want to keep your altar safe from others touching it, then make sure the cloth is large enough to fold over the objects when they are not in use or have a separate cloth that you can use for this purpose.

On your altar you can place power objects. You can add statues of spiritual or religious figures that resonate with you. Include natural objects that you've collected on walks; special gifts that have been given to you or that have personal significance can be a beautiful addition. Use whatever speaks to you. In time, you will accumulate other curios from your moon practices and various spiritual adventures.

If you have a stationary sacred space, then decorate the entire space in a way that inspires you. Add tapestries, photos, or houseplants to create ambience. Keep a special chair or throw pillow at your altar that you can rest on during your ceremonies or meditations.

How you choose to decorate is completely up to you. Choose objects based on how they make you feel, and use what calls to you—your choices don't need a logical reason! Your sacred space should inspire you to explore your magic.

When you're finished preparing your space, take a moment to set an intention. Knock on the altar three times and say:

I dedicate this as sacred space.
Where I can connect with my magic.
I am safe to explore and transform.
I am safe to dream and create.
So shall it be.

Now you're ready to begin your magical work!

CHAPTER 6

The Waning Moon

Going Within

> **Invitations of the Waning Moon:**
>
> *Let go and release what no longer serves you.*
>
> *Allow yourself to just be.*
>
> *Rest and hibernation are a form of growth.*
>
> *Make peace with the past to open the roads for the future.*

Into the darkness they go, the wise and the lovely.

—EDNA ST. VINCENT MILLAY

In this first lesson of *Lunar Alchemy*, we are in the waning phase of the moon. This is a time of parting, releasing, and recalibrating. As the moon's light recedes from the sky, we are drawn inward to explore the inner chambers of our psyche.

The energetic medicine of the Waning Moon is hibernation. The active parts of us will resist this inward call because we're on a continuous loop of *doing*. But the need for rest and recalibration are essential to our well-being.

During this moon phase you may feel tired and lethargic. Physical exhaustion and mental fatigue are typical manifestations of our active mind's resistance to the inward call. Consider what feels good for you right now. Allow instinct and intuition to lead you at this time. During this phase you must listen to your body . . . take a nap, spend time in stillness, and literally do nothing.

Stillness is scary for the fragmented self. The part of you that is fighting the stillness is the part of you that fears change. Your shadow self feeds on actions that perpetuate unconscious beliefs. On some level there is a knowing that stillness might lead to the discovery that those actions and beliefs are absurd. During stillness the unknown is being made known, which puts you in a place of choice.

And what would happen if you were compelled to make a change, a shift that would eradicate the old self and allow the luminous you to come forth?

Flip your perspective. Observe, rather than judge. Be, rather than do. Feel, rather than think. Discover, rather than figure out. Express your energy, rather than resist it.

Theme: Turning Lead into Gold

The ultimate goal of the ancient alchemist was to achieve the Great Work, or the Magnum Opus. By committing to your personal evolution you are entering into the Great Work.

You are transforming your "lead"—your rough spots, your kinks, your fears, and tarnished parts—into something more luminous than before . . . into "gold." This is the metaphorical and metaphysical meaning of the Philosophers Stone.

As you observe your life, you will discover chronic cycles and patterns that are rooted in beliefs. These beliefs are rooted in experiences throughout your life that left such a deep impression through impact or repetition that they've become your way of moving through the world.

These beliefs are impressed upon the inner self, which is the part of you that is always active, alive, and creating . . . but what it creates depends on the impressions left upon it.

In the Waning phase, we begin to explore the feedback of these beliefs, to go inward and repattern them.

Stepping into the Shadows: *Nigredo*

The first process of alchemy is called *nigredo*. This is the blackening stage, where you face the disparity between your authentic self and the fragmented self cobbled together through time, experience, and conditioning.

Jung calls this stage *Confession* and *Catharsis*. You have to face what's truly happening in your head, heart, mind, and life. Revealing the truth is a cathartic act. Facing your pain actually frees you.

Beginning with this stage can be the most daunting step in the lunar alchemy experience. Unfortunately, most of us spend our time running from our pain; we turn a blind eye to what isn't working under the illusion that it might disappear. But it never will, because you can't escape yourself. You have to face the pain, to name the problem.

As you go deeper into this process of nigredo, I want you to remember that there is no judgment, just feedback. Go forward with curiosity to observe whatever is happening.

I believe our pain leads us to our purpose because it shows us where we are in conflict with our own highest good. Pain shows us where we're constricted, where we are cutting off the flow of life and expansion. Most of us are living in the pain and feeding on the fear, and some part of us aches for change.

Through this experience, hold on to the knowledge that where there is darkness, there is light. Even within your own moments of darkness you have a spark of light within you. As you explore your personal phases along with the Moon, your inner light will grow into a fuller expression of your truth.

During the waning phase you get to become the observer of your life. You can think of this as disengaging to see things more objectively. Through observation you get a clearer picture of what blueprint you're actually living from. Now you can be honest about whatever obscures your light.

Look at things through symbolic eyes and metaphor. If every experience is a projection of your inner world, what wants to be seen there? What is hiding there? What do you own? What do you disown?

LOCATING CONSCIOUSNESS: EMBODIMENT EXERCISE

Let's begin our work in the here and now by checking in with our bodies and our breathing. The body is a barometer revealing the mental, emotional, and vibrational state. Sadly, we live in a world that keeps us disconnected from our bodies . . . we spend most of our time on autopilot.

Energetically speaking, your body is the densest part of you . . . because it is the crystallization of vibration. We spend a lot of time disconnected from our bodies, again, avoiding discomfort. Checking in with your body will show you instantly where you are resistant, and your breathing will actually show you how open you are to receiving nourishing, life-force energy.

Think about this metaphorically . . . breath is essential to life, if you are breathing shallow you're not connecting with life force. Your body is the bridge between your inner world and your outer world . . . if you're not in your body, then the real you is not present!

Breathing into the body will bridge the gap between flow and resistance, and this alone can be a life-altering process!

- Find a comfortable position. Wherever you are get comfortable. Feel the support of the ground beneath you. Keep your back soft and straight, rest your hands on your knees or let them hang loosely at your sides.

- Notice your body and begin to relax. Turn your awareness to the shape and weight of your body. Notice the sensations you feel right now. The firmness of your seat, the feeling of fabric on your skin, the gentle air moving through the room.

- Feel into your tense spots. Wherever you're holding tension, adjust yourself, relax and release. You can move if you need to. Notice where you can soften. Let this be an invitation to come into your body more.

- Feel the rhythm of your breath. Notice the gentle flow of your lungs expanding and your belly rising as you breathe in. Feel the sensation of release as you breathe out. Find your natural rhythm; allow your breath to wash through you like the ocean tides. Feel the sensation of relaxation washing over your whole body . . . breathe into all the space. Just notice what it feels like.

- Let your mind wander. Observe where your thoughts are going. Just watch as they unfold. Follow them like clouds in the sky. There's a fluffy one . . . watch it drift by. As it passes, redirect yourself back to your breath. Just observe . . . you can repeat to yourself . . . "Observing, observing, I'm just observing."

- Just be here for a moment. Observe the flow of your breath, the drifting of your thoughts, and the softness of your body. Open yourself to relaxation.

- Check in with yourself. Sink into your body again. Feel yourself seated here. Notice where you feel tight or tense. Breathe into that feeling and relax.

- Observe what comes up for you in this time of stillness. What thoughts are on repeat? What part of your body doesn't want to release? How does the rhythm of your breath change with each passing thought or feeling?

- Express deep gratitude for being in this place.

Journaling the Lunar Journey

To meet the shadow we must find an entry point. Inquiring within opens the door to the shadow. Get out your journal and take a few minutes to answer these questions.

> *Where am I right now? In my body, my mind,*
> *my emotions, and my life.*
> *What am I tired of?*
> *What am I tolerating?*
> *What frustrates me?*
> *What disappoints me?*

The answers to these questions will reveal what isn't working for you right now. With honesty and openness, you are observing the patterns that are operating in your life. Whatever shows up here clearly points to the barriers you're experiencing, the unconscious beliefs that are out picturing as reality. Now you can explore your kinks and face your resistance.

As you go through these journal exercises, you might consider: "Who's talking, anyway?"

Exploring the Shadow

When you disavow a part of yourself, and hide it from the world—either consciously or unconsciously—it becomes a shadow. In each of us the shadow self represents the icky stuff: those dark aspects we believe are not acceptable to our family, friends, and ourselves.

The shadow is the fragmented self. It exists because of a deep-seated fear of truly knowing and being who you are, rather than who you're told to be. What you negatively project onto the world is simply that part of yourself that you fear.

Shadow only has power when it is suppressed or continually disowned, and strangely enough, it's always showing us where we can heal and realign. If you can step into the stickiness of that place and dwell there for a while, you embrace the texture, dimension, and fullness of your own magic.

The Hungry Ghosts

There is a Buddhist belief called the Hungry Ghosts. The Hungry Ghosts are discarnate spirits who've died by extreme violence, tragedy, or trauma. Or, in some instances, the Hungry Ghosts are the forgotten spirits of the dead no longer venerated by their families and ancestors.

Loneliness and isolation turn the Hungry Ghosts into revenants of the past. So they roam, wander, and haunt people looking for approval, acceptance, sustenance, and peace. They mean no harm or malice; they instigate chaos and conflict in an attempt to get attention. Starved for approval, they are drawn to the life force of the living in the hopes that they too will be satisfied.

Imagine your shadow parts are the Hungry Ghosts.

At some point in your life an aspect of you was killed off, disconnected, or banished from your awareness . . . turned into a ghost. Now it desperately wants and needs your attention. All of its misconduct has been an attempt to make you aware of it. The Hungry Ghosts haunt you because they need you to offer them peace and approval.

You know a Hungry Ghost is around when:

- You feel triggered or angry.

- You are disapproving of something or someone.

- Feelings of extreme hate or resentment come to the surface.

- You want to run away, become invisible, or avoid something.

- You say "yes" when you mean "no," or vice versa.

- That person or situation you deeply despise or cannot stand keeps showing up.

- You feel out of control: this can look like depression, anger, sadness, or anxiety.

EXERCISE: MEETING YOUR HUNGRY GHOST

For this exercise you'll need your journal and an oracle deck. Oracle cards allow us to make the invisible visible. They reveal interconnected patterns of energy, intention, action, and consciousness. Oracles work because they give your Lunar Self metaphoric language to engage with: to ask and receive messages.

- I want you to become present in your body again. Be in this moment, with your thoughts, feelings, pain, and desire. Presence is always essential to making conscious choices.

- Breathe into your center and open yourself to just feeling what comes up. Become intimate with the pain, the fear, and the resistance. Recall the things you named in your journaling exercise (page 57).

- Call to mind these shadowed aspects, and imagine them as Hungry Ghosts. Born of some kind of tragedy, stuck in between realities; they are making noise to get your attention. These ghosts need to be heard and validated.

- As you contemplate your ghosts, I want you to ask for one to speak with you. Call it forward with your attention and awareness. Notice what comes up. Maybe there is a feeling, a knowing, a memory, a sensation—some clue that tips you off to the nature of this shadowed aspect.

- When you feel linked in . . .

- Begin shuffling your cards. Continue sinking deeper into this connection. When you feel ready, choose four cards and lay them out. One card for each question below. Take a few minutes to journal around what you see.

    What do you look like?
    Where did you come from?

Why are you not at peace?
How can I help you?

Forgiveness and acceptance are important to the process of releasing and integrating the Hungry Ghosts.

Weekly Waning Moon Practice

- Throughout the week, continue to be receptive to whatever is showing up for you. You've opened a door to change!

- Keep journaling on the questions you answered to locate your consciousness. These questions will help you be aware of your resistance and your patterns so you can consciously disrupt the cycle and create change.

- Notice what "ghosts" come bumping around your life and use that awareness to further soften and release.

- Recalibrate by getting plenty of rest, taking naps, going to bed early, and spending time doing NOTHING.

- Take some time each night to go outside to look at the moon or imagine her face as it diminishes into the velvety darkness.

The following suggested ceremonies can further your process.

Ceremonies of the Moon

Ceremony is a powerful tool because it engages all the parts of the self to move energetically, shift consciousness, and connect with the body. These two ceremonies are a great way to continue the process of honoring, releasing, and recalibrating.

Feeding the Hungry Ghosts: Rice Offerings

In folk traditions, the Hungry Ghosts are left offerings of food, drink, incenses, and prayer to help ease their hunger. It was believed that these spirits had tiny mouths, large bellies, and an endless hunger. So a traditional offering was uncooked rice because it's small enough to pass through their mouths and would expand in their bellies.

Looking through metaphorical eyes, you could say that a tiny gesture of kindness and understanding can begin to fill even the biggest void.

In this ceremony, you will make an offering to your Hungry Ghost. This ceremony will help you remain open and mindful of your shadowed aspects so they can be healed and reintegrated. It will also move, shift, and transmute your energetic cords and vibration.

Choose a special bowl to use for this ceremony—something large and appealing. Wash and dry it, then set it in a private place where you can do this practice.

Every day take up a small handful of rice. Hold it close to your heart and bring to mind the impression of your Hungry Ghost. Imagine expressing love, acceptance, and compassion for this spirit. Pour that feeling into the rice. You could speak out loud as you do this or silently in your mind—whatever words of acceptance are needed.

Then place this handful of rice in the bowl and repeat this affirmation or something similar:

> I nourish, honor, and accept you. I offer food, love, and good thoughts for your hunger. May you be at peace. You are released from suffering.

As you go through this process, envision yourself accepting the part of you that needs resolution, acceptance, and peace.

Do this every day until the New Moon.

You can keep your bowl of rice as a reminder of the work you've done. You might run your fingers through it as you speak to your Hungry Ghosts in the future or you might compost it to be returned to the earth.

Dissolving Blocks: Black Candle Ceremony

This candle ceremony works with the Waning Moon's energy to release. You can do this day by day along with the Hungry Ghost ceremony. I prefer to do this daily during the Waning Moon.

A candle ceremony is called sympathetic magic, meaning you are symbolically enacting something to shift the energy. As the candle's flame melts and consumes the wax, so too does the thing you are releasing become transformed and transmuted.

You will need a fresh black candle and a tool for carving (a darning needle works nice).

Call to mind whatever you are resisting and distill it down to one word or phrase.

Now inscribe the candle with that word or phrase with your tool.

Hold the candle in your hands and push all the mental and emotional energy around this topic into the candle (this process is "encoding" it).

Then light the candle and repeat this affirmation:

I let go of and fully release (the thing).

Allow the candle to burn down or snuff it out after a few minutes. Repeat each night until it has burned out.

Energetic Correspondences for the Waning Moon

Here are some correspondences for the Waning Moon phase to help you craft your own ceremonies and practices and to deepen your connection with tools you're already familiar with.

Stones and crystals:

- Black tourmaline for releasing and balancing.

- Apache tears for cleansing, mourning, and repatterning.

- Labradorite for protection and mending the energy body.

Herbs, oils, and flower essences:

- Cedar to banish and protect.

- White sage to cleanse and purge.

- Frankincense to lighten and ease.

- Aspen flower essence to ease fear of the unknown.

- Crabapple for cleansing.

- Honeysuckle to stop living in the past.

Oracle cards:

- *Lunar Nomad Oracle:* Coffin, Shears, Aura, and Bats.

- Tarot: Death, Tower, Moon, and Devil.

CHAPTER 7

The New Moon

Growing Light

Invitations of the New Moon

Right now is the right place to begin.

Even the smallest light can illuminate.

You can create anything from "nothing."

New beginnings are unfolding.

The wound is the place where light enters you.

—RUMI

During the New Moon, the moon's majesty is but a smile of light against the inky blackness of the night sky. Her light is growing, and so too is her power and presence. The New Moon is the time when the door opens for new beginnings. The light is ripe with possibilities for you to expand your consciousness, sow your seeds of intention, and learn to see life from a whole new vantage point.

In the rich and fertile womb of darkness, you've created the space for magic to spring into life. Like freshly tilled soil, your inner world is ready to be sown with seeds of intention. Over the coming weeks, as the moon gains more light, these seeds will find roots and break ground, eventually blooming into expression. Whatever intentions you sow now will be harvested later.

Holding space for the light means acknowledging the shadows. Shadow cradles light, light always creates shadow. Though possibility hangs heavy in the air, the shadows are not far behind. Going into this phase means continuing to honor the shadows and the light simultaneously.

This contrast of experience serves to show you where you are and where you'd like to be. The shadow is the gap in-between. If you flip your perspective, then shadows are no longer resistance, they are the outer boundary that lets the light grow—the womb, the container, the bridge, the outline.

Most people consider the New Moon to be the first official phase of the lunar cycle. However, in lunar alchemy it is important to make the space for a new seed of intention to be planted. We don't begin working with light to avoid the shadows; we begin working with shadows so we can fully understand the light. Any good horticulturist will tell you that proper and healthy soil is essential for thriving vegetation. Your inner space is no different.

The Waning Moon is a precarious time when you face the resistance that is holding back the light blessings in your life. At first glance this could seem counterintuitive—why would you acknowledge what you *don't* want in order to create what you do?

It's simple.

Knowing where you are now is the key to clearly moving forward. In this way the pain becomes the healer rather than the enemy. Just as physical pain can show you how you can take better care of yourself, shadow-pain can show you where you can shine the light of awareness to bring peace, understanding, and healing. Only then can you make a conscious choice to move forward and create a new life.

Over the next three weeks notice how the moon's light grows. At this time, the moon is farthest away from us down here on earth, so not only is she gaining light and clarity, she is getting closer. Your embodied light will get fuller, closer, and more expressed as time passes as well. You are like the moon; the moon lives inside of you.

The New Moon is like the first brushstroke of paint on a fresh canvas. It isn't necessary to know exactly where this creative endeavor will take you. Be open and curious as to how you're called to create and express yourself on the canvas of the sky. See this phase as the quickening. You are fertile with change and something must grow in this space.

Theme: Creative Desire Is the Seat of Magic

Now you can begin thinking about what you'd like to create. Desire is the foundation of effective magic. Whatever you desire, whatever you long for in your heart and bones, must find an outlet. A good question to ask is:

What wants to come into expression?

Desire can be fearsome for most people—it feels hot, sticky, seductive; it has many negative connotations. There's nothing inherently negative about desire. Even if that desire is leading you to choices and experiences that look negative on the surface, it is nothing more than another tango with the ghosts . . . so you can heal the disconnect and sink deeper into your truth. The desire *underneath* that desire will take you a step closer to embodying light.

You might fear your desires because you fear getting what you want. Society has conditioned us to look scornfully upon anything that might make us seem greedy or self-centered. But I'm here to tell you that you can have whatever the hell you want.

Unless your desires are fully expressed, in all your dark and light, you'll never be able to show up in this world as a force for positive change. Never shy away from what you want, even when that thing feels like you are treading deeper into shadowed lands. Once you're there, you can shine your light and dispel the darkness.

Even now, in our social and political landscape, we are facing the shadow of our collective consciousness. We're being made aware of the stain that greed, fear, domination, and oppression have left upon us. Though it can be appealing to throw stones at the supposed enemy, we're all collectively entwined in this shadow. Remember, the wound is the sliver through which the light comes in.

The New Moon is the wake-up call. She's showing you where you can heal and express simultaneously. Look at the wounds, name the desire, and let the light come in. No more sleepwalking through life!

Ask yourself: *Where can the light come in?*

Investigations into Darkness and Light: *Albedo*

The second stage of alchemy is called albedo. This is the whitening stage where the prevailing darkness is fractured by the pervasive light, eventually to be transmuted from mounds of resistance to the clay of creation. Jung calls this the *Elucidation* stage where clarity emerges.

In this moon phase, we illuminate and amplify power. It is through the shadowy specters that we discover the light and shining ones. Light is surfacing, the first inklings of the Lunar Self are present. You've made offerings to the shadowy ghosts to increase the light within.

As you open to this sense of discovery, become sensitive to and aware of the impressions of your soul emerging. The Lunar Self speaks through symbols and metaphor. Even the smallest streak of light allows wisdom and consciousness to stream in.

At this stage you begin to dismantle the chains of conditioning that have grown heavy over time. The patterns and cycles of resistance are made apparent so you can move forward with freedom. Suspend the impulse to turn away from the shadows as your light increases; this is the shadow's defense mechanism.

Your Hungry Ghosts ultimately want peace and acceptance, but they fear the unknown, the great beyond, because they fear annihilation. They don't always go easily, but you must keep going. The pain of staying the same has outgrown the fear of change. Now you can step into your power and find your luminance.

Trust your inner knowing that once your Ghosts find peace, they are transformed to light, rather than annihilated.

Light Is Cradled Among the Shadows

Just as our weakness can reveal our power, our pain can reveal our healing—shadow can reveal our light. Before moving forward, let us consider what Hungry Ghosts you faced during the waxing phase of the moon.

Remember, the shadows outline the light, so the light can be explored.

Meeting your Hungry Ghosts allows you to make conscious the impulses of the soul. By knowing where your inner world is in opposition with your outer reality, you can see the disconnection among belief, intention, and action. Whatever is revealed here becomes the foundation for changing the trajectory of your destiny.

EXERCISE: LETTING GO OF THE HUNGRY GHOSTS

- Close your eyes and begin breathing deeply. Feel whatever feelings are floating in your body, mind, and spirit.

- Give some words to these feelings. Start with fear . . . and work your way up. "I am afraid of," "I am (angry, sad, heartbroken, anxious, etc.)." Just take note of these feelings to measure the progress made on your journey.

- In your mind's eye, summon a vision of your Hungry Ghost. Begin to notice all the details of this ghost—see, feel, envision, know.

    What does your Ghost look like?
    What does your Ghost feel like?
    What does your Ghost sound like?
    Does your Ghost remind you of anything?
    Does your Ghost bring up any memories?

Maybe you are met with a looming visage of darkness that embodies your abusive relationship. Or maybe you are met by an impish figure taunting you into believing you're stuck in a dead-end job. However your Hungry Ghost appears to you, it's an apparition of your fears, not your truth.

Now, your Ghost appears to be mocking, taunting, and lurching at you. But something curious is happening—as it moves about, it becomes less threatening and more interesting. Your Ghost isn't trying to harm you . . . It's actually caught up in its own peculiar dance . . . Its cycles of existence. See it becoming a little theatrical . . . comical.

You watch closer, with more interest. You start to move with the Ghost. You are dancing the dance of your shadows. The rhythmic beat starts to move through you . . . until you are Ghost dancers in a trance together.

All Hungry Ghosts are kept alive by feeling invisible, unacknowledged, and unaccepted. Give it a chance and it will speak. Let your Ghost confide in you. Let it share its life's story. Be brave, kind. and welcoming.

Gently ask:

> *What keeps you from peace?*
> *Why do you haunt me?*
> *What made you this way?*

As your Ghost speaks, feel whatever sensations bubble up inside. Listen to its words. Let them roll deep into you.

How does your Ghost's story connect to your own?

Are you related in some way?

Recall your emotions at the beginning of this journey.

Have they shifted any?

Do you have a new perspective?

Kindly speak to your Ghost, offering words of love, kindness, and encouragement. Express compassion and remind your Ghost that whatever hurt or anger it clings to is okay, and encourage your Ghost to let it go now.

Suddenly a feeling of peace floods the space. You see your Ghost begin swaying before you. Drifting upward, it becomes a hazy cloud lodged in the frame of the sky . . . until it bursts, scatters, and dissolves into pieces.

Now in the void where it once was, a small spark of light appears. This is the light of new beginnings, seeding the darkness.

Your intentions are now becoming clearer to you. Keep an open heart and open arms, and continue to invite the light into your life. You've just stepped into the fertile grounds of the creative unknown.

When you're ready, return to the room and write down any impressions from your journey.

What wisdom did your Ghost offer you?
How can you integrate this into your life?

Meeting the Shining Ones

Energy is never created or destroyed, only transmuted—so when your Hungry Ghosts finally find peace and acceptance, they make the transition into a luminous state or become a Shining One.

In some cultures, they are called the Venerated Dead. These are the thriving spirits of those transitioned souls in the afterlife. These beings have transitioned into a higher plane of existence. No longer caught in between lives, their power and influence become balanced rather than exaggerated.

According to many African belief systems, the dead become divine, and that divinity shines on the future generations who venerate them. So they guide, protect, and work on our behalf.

In this context we speak of the Hungry Ghosts and the Shining Ones as metaphoric concepts of our own energetic fragments or psyche selves;

but these concepts can be seen as something literal and metaphoric. That is the nature of soul language.

The Shining Ones reflect the power, grace, and majesty of our own divine nature—they become the intermediaries between you and the Universe. The Shining Ones keep you aligned with your highest good so you can fulfill your soul purpose as an expression of the divine in the here and now.

Each Hungry Ghost that finds peace becomes a Shining One. But for all your shadows, you've always had light, so you've always been under the protection and care of light beings. The Shining Ones have always been there.

Can you name a time in your life where you felt divine intervention?

There is a state that I call "Spiritual Bypass." This is the state where you give up your own divine autonomy. This is a common go-to mindset among the New Age community: the idea that something did or didn't happen because the Universe made and ordained it so.

This mindset robs you of choice and possibility. Your life is yours to live, to choose, to express. When you relinquish your power of choice, you venerate the power of Fate (the idea that the future is fixed) making life happen to you.

However, the future is fluid, you create your destiny, and your destiny is determined by your choices now. This doesn't negate the existence of a higher power or other beings in the Universe working for or against you, but it does change the playing field.

What if you change "I'm leaving it up to the Universe" to "I'm leaving it up to my own inner wisdom"?

Lunar Alchemy

What if you change "It wasn't meant to be" to "I wasn't ready"?

Whatever divine intervention you've received happened *because* of you—on some level you summoned it, you created it, you allowed it. You hold the key to your destiny.

Shadow work has shown you how pain can take you to your edge. You've witnessed the proof of your resistance and limiting beliefs. This isn't only true for the "negative," but the positive experiences or blessings in your life are also proof of wanting and allowing. It is cosmic law.

The Shining Ones are the light around you, and the light within you. They are the living creation of your personal mastery.

You know a Shining One is around when:

- You feel safe, guided, and clear.

- Blessings and miracles appear.

- Synchronicities lead you to something big.

- You feel good, positive, and well.

- Things just flow.

- Healing and forgiveness take place.

- A sense of grace comes over you.

- You can observe without reacting.

EXERCISE: EXPERIENCING LIGHT MEDITATION

When you experience your own light, you experience your own power. Let's go into the mystery to find your light-blessings.

- I want you to close your eyes and get comfortable. Feel the safe and secure space beneath you, supporting you, holding you, embracing you.

- Feel your body relax. Let all your tightness and tension fade away. Move if you need to. Allow yourself to unwind.

- Begin breathing. Take a deep breath in and feel your belly expand. Exhale and feel your belly fall. Like ocean waves, allow your natural rhythm to lull you deeper. The ebbing and flowing of your breath.

- Continue to let go and release into this place. You are safe to relax. This time is a gift—you have nowhere else to be, nothing else to do. Be present.

- Begin to see yourself floating . . . floating in a soft, warm, inky darkness. Everything around you is dark, luscious, and comforting. You feel a sense of peace and safety here.

- Feel the gentle caress of the dark washing over your body. Continue to breathe. With each breath, you are falling deeper into peace, letting go of everything . . . there's nothing but this moment, this feeling of tranquility. You're in this protective womb of fluid darkness.

Lunar Alchemy

- Become aware of your surroundings—there is a prevailing darkness all around you. You feel safe, curious, and receptive. Just be here for a moment: floating, receiving, being.

- As you continue to relax, a feeling starts to stir within you, that curious feeling of something emerging . . .

- You notice a little flick of light cradled in the darkness ahead of you . . .

- You feel drawn to the light . . . it beckons you closer . . . gently you swim nearer to this light . . . it feels magnetic . . . without effort you find yourself getting closer, and closer . . .

- Suddenly you emerge from the surface of an inky pool of water. The air around you is sweet with the scent of jasmine . . . you feel warmed and euphoric . . . every cell in your body feels relaxed and at peace.

- The bead of light is now a glowing orb above you, shining down from the velvety sky.

- Now the bead of light that beckoned you closer is a glowing orb draped within the folds of velvety night sky above you.

- Feel this light . . . soft, sweet, relaxing . . . feel this light soothe you, ease your doubts and fears . . . feel this light awaken something within you.

- Be here for a moment, bathed in the light. Notice how light feels to you . . . notice what the light awakens within you . . . just be.

- Begin to notice your breathing again. Notice how you feel in your body . . . notice what sensations and emotions well up within you . . .

- As you become present within your body, you notice your own skin is glowing brightly, you are luminescent . . .

- Suddenly you realize the light in the sky is your own reflection. You've found your light . . . you're glowing in the dark . . .

- When you're ready, come back to the room.

Journaling the Lunar Journey

Journal on these two questions:

What does light feel like to me?
When do I feel lit up?

EXERCISE: MEETING YOUR SHINING ONES

For this exercise, you'll need your journal and an oracle deck. Oracle cards allow us to make the invisible, visible. They reveal interconnected patterns of energy, intention, action, and consciousness. Oracles work because they give your Lunar Self metaphoric language to engage with: to ask and receive messages.

- I want you to become still and present. Be here in this moment. Open yourself to receiving whatever needs to come through at this time. Trust your process.

- Become aware of the light in and around you. Recall your experiences with the nature of light during your guided journey. Keep breathing into that feeling and allow the light to grow and expand around you.

- Silently invite your Shining Ones to be with you. Imagine that they are near. Feel the warmth, comfort, and support they radiate. Be open to the grace and bright blessings they'd like to share with you.

- Now ask one to step forward. Notice what comes up for you. Whatever is happening in your head and heart. Be aware of the thoughts, feelings, sensations, and memories that might surface.

- When you feel the connection . . .

- Begin shuffling your cards. Continue sinking deeper into this connection. When you feel ready. Choose four cards and lay them out, one card for each question below. Take a few minutes to journal about it.

  How do you appear to me?
  What light are you helping me grow?
  What do I need to know about my own light?
  How can I honor your?

Grace and gratitude will help you move into a deeper communion with the Shining Ones.

Weekly New Moon Practice

- Continue to journal on your Ghosts and Shining Ones.

- Use the question: Is this growing my light or feeding my shadows?

- Notice what oracular messages or signs appear in your life.

- Write down any dreams you have over the coming week.

- Be curious to new adventures and opportunities—get out of your comfort zone.

- Spend time feeding your creativity.

- Go outside and look at the moon!

Ceremonies of the Moon

Nourishing the Shining Ones: Floral Water Offerings

As you deepen your connection with the Shining Ones, you can cool and nourish them with offerings of floral water. By offering floral water to them, you encourage sweet connection and nourish the growing relationship forming between you.

Floral waters hold a cool, sweet, and soothing vibration. Making these offerings will not only increase the connection you have to the Shining Ones, but it will increase your own glow of vitality and attraction.

Use a clear glass cup or bowl for your offerings. You can simply float a few fresh rosebuds or flower petals in spring water or you can purchase a special hydrosol such as rose water, orange blossom water, or jasmine water.

Begin each evening that you spend with the New Moon by making your floral water offering to the Shining Ones. You can make this offering at your special altar or shrine used for all your spiritual work.

Hold your cup or bowl of water in both hands. Breathe deeply, relaxing and connecting with your intention. Feel the Shining Ones drawing near. Let the sweet floral scent of the water fill your awareness. Blow into the water three times and say:

I offer this water to the Shining Ones.
I acknowledge your presence.
I express gratitude for your blessings.
With peace and love.
So shall it be.

Leave your water offering on your altar.

Each evening, you can blow into the same cup of floral water and repeat the words above. You do not need to replace the water each time, unless you feel called to. At the end of the New Moon, you can use the offering to water a plant or pour it outside near a flower or tree.

You can continue to make offerings to the Shining Ones each moon phase if you feel drawn to the practice. If you choose to keep this as a daily practice, refresh your water offering each week or when the water has evaporated or no longer appears fresh.

Sweet Things: Honey Jar Ceremony

Honey has a long history in magic and mythology. It has been called the food of the gods because of its sweet and sensuous nature. Some cultures regard bees as the messengers of the divine because of the ecological role they play as pollinators. Honey holds the energetic medicine of sweetness, abundance, vitality, and beauty.

In folk magic, honey is used to sweeten life, to attract positive influence, and to draw in desires. A touch of honey to the tongue while speaking someone's name is said to make them sweet to you in turn, and dabbing a bit of honey on the wrists is said to make you more alluring.

With the New Moon, you will plant a seed of intention to draw your desires into life. A powerful intention begins with a feeling. What desires can you name right now in your life? What would attaining each of those desires make you feel?

If you can highlight the feeling and let go of the form, you allow the creative forces of the Universe to create situations that support more of that feeling. That may look very different from the original desire, but the feeling is amplified nonetheless.

On a sheet of paper, make a list of your desired feelings. What would you like to feel right now in your life?

Summon those feelings into your body and feel them radiate outward. Like a magnet, you are pulling those feelings into your life. Begin folding the paper in half, folding it toward you. Repeat this fold three times.

Hold the honey jar close to your heart, pour your desired feelings into the jar, and say:

Golden honey, draw all good things near.
Golden honey, make life sweeter.
Blessings of the Shining Ones.
My desires now come to me.
So shall it be.

Open the honey and taste a little bit of its golden sweet flavor. Close the lid tightly and tape your slip of paper to the bottom of the jar. Place the jar on a tray or plate and surround it with flower petals, plants, crystals, and other trinkets or talismans that feel good.

Every day of the New Moon, open the jar, taste just a little bit of the honey, and say:

Golden honey, draw all good things near.
Golden honey, make life sweeter.
Blessings of the Shining Ones.
My desires now come to me.
So shall it be.

If you'd like, you can burn a white candle inscribed with your desired feeling next to your honey jar to add and increase the light.

Working with Water to Clear and Bless

Bathing can become a staple ceremony to awaken the connection between inner and outer worlds. By submerging your body in water filled with herbs, oils, and other ingredients, you can infuse your aura with specific energy and intention.

During the New Moon, you're working to clarify your intention and point of attraction. To support this intention you can perform a cleansing bath to clear away any lingering energies that are clouding your perception. A blessing bath will amplify your vibration so your intention takes shape quicker.

Bathing rituals are usually done in a series, over a set amount of time. For example you could take a bath at the start and end of a moon phase or for a series of days: 3 days, or 7 days, or 9 days. Align your bathing rituals with the moon phases, seasons, or other special occasions. But I always encourage you to trust when you feel guided to do this.

To prepare a bath simply:

- Fill a tub or bowl with warm water.

- Place your materials into the bath.

- Pray over the bath from the heart with your intention (blessing or cleansing).

- And pray this intention during the bath.

A SPIRITUAL CLEANSING BATH

This is a sea salt cleansing bath. Sea salt draws out and neutralizes "negative" energies gathered throughout the day, heavy thought patterns, and troubled emotions.

To prepare a cleansing bath, run a tub of warm water. Add a handful of sea salt while saying:

Spirit of salt, bless this bath.
Clear away heavy energies.
May I be buoyant and luminous.
So shall it be.

Now slip into the bath and submerge yourself fully. Make sure to get your whole body wet, including your head. Cup the salt water in your hands and rub your entire body with a downward swooping motion. This loosens debris in your aura.

Soak for about 15 minutes. Stay in the tub while you let the water drain away. As it drains, imagine all lingering energies going along with it. Quickly shower afterward. Then towel dry, and dress in something clean and comfortable.

A FLORAL BLESSING BATH

For this blessing bath, you will use the nourishing power of flowers to enrich your aura with high vibration. You can choose any flowers that are available. Roses are wonderful and easy to find. White roses or flowers in particular symbolize increasing light.

Run a warm bath of water. Remove the flower heads from the stem and gather them in a bowl. Begin adding the flowers to the water while saying:

Sacred flowers that bloom and unfold.
Increase my light and help it grow.
So shall it be.

Slip into the bathwater and give yourself time to relax. Envision yourself being filled with delicate energy. Imagine yourself unfurling in the warm embrace of the water. Make sure to submerge your entire body, including your head. Cup water in your hands and sweep the water upward over your body, drawing blessings to you.

When you are finished, towel dry and dress in something clean and comfortable.

I suggest doing a cleansing bath at the beginning of the New Moon and follow with a blessing bath the next day or at the end of this phase.

Energetic Correspondences for the New Moon

Here are some correspondences for the New Moon phase to help you craft your own ceremonies and practices and to deepen your connection with tools you're already familiar with.

Stones and crystals:

- Selenite to increase light in the body, mind, and spirit.

- Moonstone to connect with the moon's phases.

- Ametrine to connect with inner wisdom and open channels.

Herbs, oils, and flower essences:

- Rose for love and sweetness.

- Orange for vitality and strength.

- Lavender for peace and serenity.

- Clematis to stay present.

- Water violet to stop isolation.

Oracle cards:

- *Lunar Nomad Oracle:* Pathways, Heart, Ring, and Child.

- Tarot: Fool, Temperance, High Priestess, and Chariot.

CHAPTER 8

The Waxing Moon

Illuminating the Path

> Invitations from the Waxing Moon:
>
> *Possibilities are ripe and ready to be tasted.*
>
> *Intention met with action creates reality.*
>
> *Shadow and light are at equal standing.*
>
> *Bridge between dream and reality.*
>
> *Action, action, action!*
>
> *What are you ready to do?*

You have to find what sparks a light in you so that you in your own way can illuminate the world.

—OPRAH WINFREY

Luna is in her waxing phase, and she is half light and half shadow. This is a phase of embodying light and moving into change. You've made the unconscious impulses conscious by working with your Hungry Ghosts, and now you're inviting the Shining Ones to come forward and usher you into a new life. You've summoned and conjured deeply held feelings and desires, and now you begin to notice the proof of possibilities around you.

Now these possibilities hang heavy on the vine, like glittering moon fruit, ripening each day, and beckoning you to taste their delicious, sweet juices. Each one has a unique and tantalizing flavor—something you've never experienced before. Get curious about which possibility calls to you. They're all right here for you to savor. One by one if you like.

The Waxing Moon invites you into your power and shows you how to receive. You're receiving light and being filled from the inside out. Like the moon, you are growing and glowing into a fuller, more embodied expression. An expression of the power and presence that has been, and always will be, available to you.

As your light grows, your life is transformed, and you continue to release and allow. At times you'll want to push through the process, wrangle yourself into transformation, but Luna invites you into the allowing. She shows you how to make peace with your Ghosts and honor your Shining Ones with ease.

At this time, you could feel tired, irritable, rushed, and confused. You could have ups and downs, times when you feel totally inspired and energized, then bottom out and need to rest. You're seeking equilibrium between light and dark right now. The moon's message is to forget about "doing" in the dominant, controlling sense. You can and will take steps and actions to move forward, but being is enough.

Theme: Accessing the Power of Choice

With a flip of perspective, choices become nothing more than flow or resistance. There is no right choice or wrong choice, there is just choosing or not choosing, to be conscious to the impulse or to continue sleepwalking through life. Ease, soften, allow, receive; just flow. That is CHOICE.

We are at the bridge between dreams and reality. When a dream becomes full enough, it spills over into reality. An embodied dream is an intention that moves into action, and actions create change. Always going back to the knowing that you don't have to fight or force, just being is enough to become.

Like the moon, effortlessly move into your light.

Conflict between the inner and outer world will crop up during this phase. Your old self, your Hungry Ghosts, fear the light, because they fear annihilation. They do not know the warm liberation of the light. But you know that there is freedom hanging in the glow of the moon.

Resistance and pain are a step toward evolution. This phase can create hurdles for you to get past. Your old self, your collected self, will be adamant about staying in the inbetween. It feels safer there, because once you cross the point of no return, the whole "game" changes.

Pay attention to the signs and messages offered by your Ghosts. They will continue showing you your resistance and fear. As you notice your kinks and rigid edges, you'll see where you're holding back your light!

Raising the Light: *Citrinatas*

In alchemy, this moon phase corresponds to citrinatas, the yellowing or raising the light. According to Jung, this is the *Education* phase, where you see new ways of being. You're bringing the light into reality, substantiating the true self, and acknowledging the gifts that are enrobed in light.

Don't confuse the process of embodying your light with the idea of perfection. Lunar alchemy is the process of shattering the old self, the collected self, and moving the shadow self into the light. You're becoming who you've always been, not something else. You are discovering your truth—the raw, sexy, glittering, dangerous truth of who you really are, beyond the conditions, the responsibilities, the fear, and the pain.

As you explore these inner chambers of yourself, you rouse the light cradled within. You're actually invoking your own powerful self to manifest. This is the key to unlocking the transformation process. It all starts with the choice *to be*.

Journaling the Lunar Journey

What are you still tolerating in your life?

What are you avoiding?

What do you not want to face, do, say?

How are you choosing not to choose?

What part of your is being validated by this?

- Imagine floating in an expansive pool of soothing, tranquil waters. The light of the moon dances on the surface. Your body feels weightless and supported.

- You're lying comfortably in the embrace of a large lotus blossom. You close your eyes and ease into this space. The soft petals embrace every part of your body; your breathing becomes calm and rhythmic. You relax deeper into this space . . .

- Here in this moment you are safe. You trust the tranquil waters . . . the womb of your lotus flower . . . the healing light of the moon above. You trust that you're in process . . . being and becoming all at once.

- You sense movement beneath you. A gentle pulse . . . the water swaying, ebbing, and flowing. You feel yourself moving. You are allowing . . . you are receiving . . . being and receiving.

- Your lotus blossom begins moving tranquilly down stream . . . effortlessly riding the waves . . . Your senses tingle. You're filled up with joy . . . with comfort . . . with healing . . . with a keen sense of knowing . . . that all is well, all is right.

- Your lotus blossom continues moving . . . flowing . . . effortlessly caressing each wave and bend in the river. You allow yourself to be rocked and cradled by this movement . . . for a while . . . just flowing, being, becoming . . .

- Now when you're ready to come back to the room . . . knowing that you're still in the flow . . . being . . . allowing . . . receiving . . .

- You're invited to ponder:

  How do I receive?
  How does it feel to receive?

Grace Unfolding

During the Waxing Moon your Lunar Self will be more awake and aware. Divine guidance, intuitive hits and direction will come more frequently. These impressions will lead you to the clear knowing that the illuminated pathway before you is the direction forward. No need to do or try, just be, and begin to notice.

In this knowing is a profound message. Spirit wishes you to know that being your whole self, begin fully expressed in the world, isn't a luxury. This is a necessity. The only way to thrive is to be unapologetically you. Choose it now, live it now, be it now!

Regardless of how your Hungry Ghosts will try to seduce you—with fear, doubt, guilt, or shame—continue to feel your light. Everything you want and need is right here. Allow yourself to come fully into the world.

You might notice during this phase that the moon appears during the daylight hours. Her message to you is: stop hiding in the dark; bring yourself into the light of day!

Working Your Light

"We're desperate to give ourselves labels and titles, yet petrified that these identities will give the wrong impression. We're afraid to be seen and afraid not to be seen— equally scared to be somebody and nobody."

—GABRIELLE ROTH

Let me defuse any resistance. Lunar alchemy isn't about letting go of who you are or losing any part of your identity. You're excavating the darkness to find the light . . . this emerging light is your authentic self, your truth . . . the real soul that's always been inside.

This work can feel painful, like you are losing part of your identity. Sometimes it will feel like a type of death. You're actually dissolving the collected self. The collected self is the part of you reared on conditioning, forged in the cacophony of voices, and containing inherited beliefs encountered throughout your life.

For most of us, we've confused our collected self as our authentic self. You see this in the different roles and responsibilities placed upon you. You feel pressured to be something to others, before yourself. This phase invites you to drop the juggling act of disparate identities, so you can discover exactly who you are at the core.

These discoveries will come moment to moment because in each moment you get to choose the next step, the next movement, and the next impression gifted to you from your inner wisdom. Each tiny step linked together makes up the whole journey. You don't need to figure anything out—just allow yourself to discover.

Isn't it exciting that you no longer have to live a static life? You are moving, swirling, and unfolding energy. You get to shape-shift through this world and try on all the different facets of your inner form. You're unshackling your truth!

EXERCISE: LIGHT-READING

Light cast through a prism can take on many different textures, colors, and expressions. Let's work your light by looking at the possibilities.

- Pull out your oracle cards. Hold them to your heart center. Become still and open. Allow yourself to be in this moment. Just breathe into your awareness, your deep knowing.

- Become aware and perceptive of the space around you. Set the intention that you are in sacred space, surrounded by the love and protection of the Shining Ones.

- Repeat this invocation:

  I acknowledge and awaken the light within me. I ask for your wisdom and insight. With the protection and guidance of the Shining Ones I now choose to work my light.

See, sense, feel your light enter the cards. Connect with ancient and profound spirit language. Shuffle the deck, holding the intention in your heart that you're invoking your light.

When you are ready, choose a card for each question:

What form does my light wish to take?

How can I move into this expression of my light?

What is supporting this expression now?

What is obscuring this expression of my light?

What else should I know?

Open yourself to whatever insight pours forth through the cards. Drink in the wisdom and energy medicine of each card and journal about your experience.

EXERCISE: THE GLITTERING PATH FORWARD

Empowered with light, you can see the glittering path forward. You're ready to unleash your magic. Start where you are right now, and choose your next step.

Remember: Intention + Action = Conscious Change.

Journaling the Lunar Journey

In your journal answer:

What one step can I take right now to work my light?

This could be an action, an internal shift, a practice, etc.

Make a list with two columns. One column will be:

"Actions to work my light this week."

The other column will be:

"Obstacles that could keep me from working my light."

Weekly Waxing Moon Practice

- Set an intention each day and take an action toward that intention.

- Notice what oracular messages appear in your life.

- Write down any dreams you have over the coming week.

- Continue to be curious to new adventures, opportunities, and commit to getting out of your comfort zone.

- Spend time feeding your creativity.

- Go outside and look at the moon!

Ceremonies of the Moon

Plumes of Intention: Daily Incense Devotional

Incense spans magical and spiritual traditions. Since ancient times, herbs, minerals, and resins have been burned for a multitude of magical purposes: to clear a space, to draw in blessings, to carry prayers, to feed the gods.

Incense engages the senses and conjures powerful energy. Incense draws on the inherent magic of botanicals and the alchemical process of transmutation to effect change.

A simple ceremony to help you embody your light and feed your intention is to perform a daily incense devotional.

You can work with whatever incense feels right to you. Frankincense is a wonderful resin used by many spiritual paths, which lifts the hold of depression and anxiety. Choose incense that is sweet, warm, and inviting. Incense in the form of stick or cone works well for this process because they need little supervision, and they serve a dual purpose by also acting as a timer.

You can perform your devotion in the morning or evening (trust your own intuition). Find a comfortable place where you can spend time in contemplation—maybe put a pillow on the floor or sit on a comfy chair. Have a fireproof incense burner, your chosen incense, and a lighter (you can do this at your altar with the rest of your work).

Ground, center, and become aware of your body. Relax and breathe into any tension you're holding on to. Allow yourself to come into this present moment. Now begin to call upon your light and focus on the intention that you're working on creating in your life.

Hold that intention deep in your heart-space. Light the incense and say:

With this incense I nurture my light.
With this incense I honor the Shining Ones.
With this incense I work my light.
With this incense my intentions are made real.

Now imagine your intentions are a blooming rose growing from your heart center. Imagine the plumes of smoke unfurling and carrying your desired intention out into the ethers, out into the Universe to be made manifest in whatever way is necessary.

Just be here for a while, with the feeling, with the intentions, and immersed in devotion to growing your light.

Energy Medicine Window: A New Way to Use Oracles

Oracle cards are a beautiful tool for seeing the patterns and stories of energy. But they are more than a fluid language to communicate with Spirit. The oracles can be used as transmitters of vibrational-energy medicine.

You can think of the cards as a window, a doorway, or an access point to a certain vibration. Combined together, you can create a more defined frequency or medicine point.

To access this energy, you can place the oracle cards on your body, like you would a crystal or a warm compress. Or you can lay them in a circle and curl up in the center, tuck them under your pillow, or just meditate on their images.

To create an energy medicine window you will need to have your oracle cards and a sacred space to work in. Choose a space where you can play with seating position and card layout.

Ground, center, and become present. Invoke your light and invite the Shining Ones to be present. Take your time just moving into the rhythm of breathing and being.

Begin to shuffle the cards. And in your mind or out loud ask:

What energy medicine do I need now?

Pull a card and lay it in front of you. Meditate on the image. Feel the vibration and frequency the card emits. Don't worry about interpreting the card or finding a meaning. That isn't the point of this ceremony. Just feel whatever the card is transmitting for you.

You can place this card on your body if you'd like. Place it on a chakra or body part that is in need. Place it near your heart. You could work with this card for the entire day by keeping it in your pocket, placing it under your pillow as you sleep, or placing it under your dish to charge your food/drink with the energy.

You could go further by choosing three more cards. Placing them around your initial card like moonbeams radiating outward.

Choose one card each for:

Body

Mind

Spirit

Now you have a larger, more defined medicine window. This can become an altar itself. You can work here, play here, meditate here, or pray here. Whatever you feel called to do—just allow this window to transmit the frequency you need.

Over time, you might work your medicine window intuitively, pulling cards and laying them out in whatever arrangement feels right. You can add other elements to the window to form an intricate mandala of energy.

Energetic Correspondences for the Waxing Moon

Here are some correspondences for the Waxing Moon phase to help you craft your own ceremonies and practices and to deepen your connection with tools you're already familiar with.

Stones and crystals:

- Citrine to open the path.

- Tigereye to ease anxiety and stimulate action.

- Carnelian for motivation, strength, and tenacity.

Herbs, oils, and flower essences:

- Rosemary to help focus, clarity, and mental fluidity.

- Lavender for peace and patience, to trust the process.

- Patchouli because it draws in whatever you desire.

- Cerato to ease distrust and promote decisiveness.

- Elm to keep a balanced sense of responsibility.

Oracle cards:

- *Lunar Nomad Oracle*: Rider, Tree, Sun, Anchor, and Lilies.

- Tarot: Empress, Magician, Chariot, and Temperance.

CHAPTER 9

The Full Moon

I AM Light

Invitations from the Full Moon:

Embodied light and unfolding light.

A time of harvest.

Full bloom and full expression.

Proof and evidence.

Witness, receive, pivot, and align.

Where are you now?

As we let our light shine, we unconsciously give other people permission to do the same. As we are liberated from our own fear, our presence actually liberates others.

—MARIANNE WILLIAMSON

Luna is in her full expression. Burning brightly in the night sky, the Full Moon pours down her power and potential. She beckons you into your own knowing and allows you to see how you've worked your light over the past three weeks. This is a good time to sit with yourself and become curious about what you have, to this point, birthed through the light through all phases of the moon.

The Full Moon completely embodies lunar magic and shows us how to do the same. As you feed your light, you become fuller, more outwardly expressed, and ready to bring your gifts to the world. This is an inward journey out.

At this time, the gravitational pull of the moon is strongest, stirring the tides, rousing the psyche, and drawing out power. Typically, you might feel anxious, raw, supercharged, and bouncing. You might even feel overstimulated. Through the lunar alchemy experience, you should feel an immense sense of knowing and certainty about your next steps forward.

The Full Moon has been considered one of the most powerful phases in many different cultures and traditions. The power of the witch was said to be at its greatest during this moon. The moon's gifts of empowerment literally pour down through the moonbeams to be soaked into the lining of your skin and the depths of your spirit.

As above, so below—you have bloomed into a new iteration of your most latent potential.

In the previous phases, you've released, created space, and called in new energies; ultimately you were asking a question, and now the Full Moon brings the answer.

Through this process, you've made the unconscious conscious by identifying attachments still lingering in the shadows and finding pockets of light folded within. This level of your experience can feel like a vacuum sucking you backward because you're not used to standing fully bathed in all your power and glory.

But this is not a time to move backward, to undo the enchantment you've woven. Let the ripe energy of the moon keep you crackling with life—stay awake!

The energy conjured now reaches a climax. This is called a "Cone of Power" where intention and energy are built, conjured, and directed through ceremony and internal awareness; swirling, building, and vibrating into a beam of light until it reaches a crescendo where it launches into the world of shape and form.

What have you conjured with the light of the moon?

Theme: Magnifying the Light

Imagine the moon as a magnifying glass. She radiates, intensifies, and pushes light into life. Something must be born now. However that manifestation takes form, know that your desires have created some tangible experience. Use the moon's influence as a lens to shine light on your present situation and clarify your point of focus.

You can also think of the Full Moon as a mirror that is completely lit. Center yourself into your awareness and connect with the core intention of consciously creating the life you want. Lunar alchemy is an experience of waking up to deliberately work with creation. To deliberately create, you must notice the proof or feedback each step of the way.

Now you can see the bigger picture—no more hazy and ambiguous edges. You've come to a clear threshold in your experience. Take note of your coordinates, consider what you're still carrying, and deliberately choose what you'd like to carry forward into your next phase of lunar alchemy. And decide what you'd like to let fade into the fuzzy darkness.

Look for the proof of your process, your deliberate choices, your openness, and your magic working. Honor the brave work you've done. Release whatever no longer serves you so you can fully embrace the new. Let the remaining fragments be recycled into the Universe. Now you can pass through the threshold.

Your intuition will pulse with insight. You're filled with awareness and creative impulses. Something will nudge you forward.

Hello New World: *Rubedo*

The fourth stage of alchemy is called rubedo, or the reddening. Red like blood pulsing—things are now brought to life. There is a union between the ephemeral and the physical. Energy and intention are made manifest.

Jung calls this stage *Transformation*. You've undergone a spiritual process of dissolving barriers, distilling your light, and now your intention coagulates, or "becomes real."

Through the light, you've birthed a physical expression of your deeply held intention. This isn't the end; it's another stone on the pathway forward—you're always moving, flowing, and unfolding.

Healing tender spots in the form of your Hungry Ghosts and finding the blessings of the Shining Ones, you now hold in your hand a gleaming jewel of power that can carry you into unknown places. Your transformation is evident because your life will look a little different than when you started, and internally you won't feel the same.

The rubedo stage is marked by physical expressions of your new eternal dynamic. You've freed yourself in some way. Your eyes are wide open now. Blinders are removed, and you're aware of your existence on a deeper, more nuanced level. This stage of transformation is the departure to a new life. You've crossed the point of no return.

The wisdom and clarity you've gained up to this point will never leave you. You will have moments of forgetfulness and sometimes you'll drift off just a little. But the deep slumber of disempowerment has been broken. Now feel the electric light of your own spirit and know that will never leave you again.

Keep feeling the electric light pulse through your veins. It moves through you, coursing through every aspect of your existence until it breaks free into the real world. Feel yourself flush with empowerment. Be receptive enough to know where magic wants to take you next.

Journaling the Lunar Journey

Writing exercise: "Freedom in Action." Answer the following questions:

Where am I free?

What will I do with this freedom?

How does freedom scare me?

How does freedom excite me?

Rite of Passage through the Moon

The Full Moon is a rite of passage. The path behind you is illuminated so you can acknowledge how far you've come, though you don't need to get caught in the tangles of the past. Here in this moment you stand at a threshold, a doorway to a new stage of life.

This rite of passage is the opportunity to acknowledge where you are at this moment, where you've come from. Most importantly you see what you can part with now to lighten your load and move forward. Deliberately choose things that serve you.

You are beckoned to step through this threshold into another lunation. This is a rendezvous with empowerment, grace, and awareness. You are waking up to the knowledge that you are the dreamer of your reality. Aligned with immense lunar power, your perspective expands to see the possibilities and opportunities over the resistance and hurdles.

Are you ready to cross the threshold?

Make a pact with your dreams. Sink deep into the moon's reflective surface and merge all that you really are, inside and out. The old version of your life is nothing but a memory; you're now breaking through to a whole different expression of yourself.

Notice what is breaking away, crumbling, and falling apart as you bloom into your full expression of light. You're uncovering something essential—a pocket of power to sustain you.

Journaling the Lunar Journey

Writing exercise: "Seeing the Milestones." In your journal, take time to write about your experience over the past three weeks of lunar alchemy and focus on answering the following questions:

What significant insights have I had?

What's been brought to light about my life, my beliefs, my experiences and desires?

How would I describe this milestone in my spiritual evolution?

What has this shown me about my personal power?

Where the Light Leads

Charged by the Full Moon, you get to experience the full spectrum of your personal power. Answering the call of your magic feels like alignment, vitality, and assurance. Resisting that call feels like discord, deprivation, and anxiety.

You feel a magnetic pull drawing your forward. You can step through the doorway into possibilities. Your power is calling you—will you answer?

MEDITATION EXERCISE: EMBRACING THE MOONLIGHT

You are about to embark on a sacred journey to greet the light and receive some form of guidance.

- Close your eyes and get comfortable. Find a seated position with your back straight. Feel the ground beneath you supporting you, holding you, cradling you in place.

- Begin to relax your body. Breathe into any tightness and resistance. Inhale relaxation and exhale release.

- Repeat this for a few breaths. Each time go deeper, relaxing more, and falling into this journey.

- As you relax into this moment, give yourself permission to receive the gift of going deeper. Deeper into the journey . . . the feeling of relaxation . . . the allowing.

- Find yourself in a beautiful room. It feels safe, sacred, cozy, and insulated from the chaos of the outside world. You feel like you're somewhere outside of time.

- You hear a gentle whooshing sound, followed by a soft crashing. It sounds like waves licking the shore. It feels so soothing to hear this ebbing and flowing around you.

- All around you are tapestries of vivid color; glittering jewels line the domed ceiling, casting iridescent light around the space. Soothing blue flames bob gently on the tip of pure white candles and plumes of smoke gather around this sacred chamber like a rising pillar of light stretching to the sky.

- You notice you are seated in an ornately carved throne, glittering with silver filigree, moonstones, opals, and intricate designs that move around the arms of the throne, and snake up the back like serpents.

- Sink deeper into the embrace of fluffy, down-filled pillows and the warmth of soft silk velvet draped around you.

- You take the whole room in, wonder by wonder. Elated by the sense of mystery and awe that fills you. You are curious about this place, and the magic it holds.

- The scent, the sound, everything around you takes you deeper into tranquility.

- You notice two beams of light cascading across the floor to either side of the throne . . . contrasting against the dark pattern of the wool rug covering the floor.

- You grow curious about the source of this light. So you stand up from the throne to see what's behind you.

- Following the sliver of light, you trace it to a large tapestry woven with ruby red pomegranates on a background of golden yellow.

- The tapestry hangs loosely between two framing pillars, and the light floods through the space where the tapestry hangs.

- A slight breeze moves through the cracks and the tapestry lightly sways in front of you . . .

- You walk closer to the tapestry. The sound of water gets louder. You reach out your hand, and pull the tapestry back . . .

- On the other side is a moonlit ocean. Waves sparkle and dance as they glide through the light of the Full Moon above . . .

- You feel wide open, awake with wonder. Something inside of you feels home.

- Gazing at the moon and the ocean and feeling this sense of inspiration, a message comes . . .

- Some oracular message appears to you here. Through the moon you're given insight.

- You see, sense, hear, know, or experience something—a vision, a manifestation, a sign—whatever comes is exactly right.

- Be here for a while . . .

- When you're ready, thank the moon and come back to this place.

   What will you do with this knowing?
   What is this message leading you to?

 ## ORACLE CARD EXERCISE: REFLECTING BY MOONLIGHT

During the Full Moon, you can ground, center, and connect with the present moment to witness the wisdom and insight present in your evolution. This exercise opens you up more to embody the light and the gifts manifested through your work. And you can get a sense for your next level of growth.

- Hold you oracle deck. Breathe into your body; find a sense of rhythm with each breath. Become calm, still, relaxed. Open yourself up to receive guidance and clarity. Feel yourself shifting into a receptive state.

- Hold your oracle deck to your heart and say:

  I open myself to clarity and guidance.
  I allow myself to receive.
  I invite my inner wisdom to speak.

- Hold your oracle deck to your forehead and say:

  I see beyond the boundaries of my finite senses.
  I look through lunar eyes.
  I confirm with lunar knowing.

- Shuffle the cards to fill them with your energy. Ponder this past lunation. Whatever comes up in your head and heart is perfect. Let it flow through.

- When you're ready, choose a card for each question:

  Where am I now?
  What is in full light?
  What is available to me now?
  What should I call in?

How can I walk through the threshold?

Is there anything else to know that can serve me?

Record your answers to these questions in your journal.

Weekly Full Moon Practice

- Do a daily inventory of your emotions, urges, and invitations.

- Pay attention to any oracular messages throughout the day.

- Write down any dreams you have over the coming week.

- What is your light showing you today?

- Be active! Dance, sing, go on adventures, create something—move energy.

- Go outside and look at the moon!

Ceremonies of the Moon

Drawing Down the Moon

> *Whenever ye have need of anything,*
> *Once in the month, and when the moon is full,*
> *Ye shall assemble in some desert place...*
> *Its deepest secrets, them my mother will*
> *Teach her, in truth all things as yet unknown.*
> *And so ye shall be free in everything...*

—ARADIA: GOSPEL OF THE WITCHES IN 1899

In her full expression, the moon has shone light on many sacred seekers from all facets of time, space, and tradition. Believed to be the embodiment of the mother goddess, the Full Moon has been honored, praised, and called down to heal, empower, and bless those who seek the light.

The witches of Tuscany honored the Full Moon as the face of Diana. They would gather at night in sacred celebration to sing, dance, feast, and show respect for the moon's blessings and for one another.

In those celebratory gatherings they would draw down the moon, calling light into their body, mind, and spirit to nourish every aspect of their being.

You can draw down the moon to nourish yourself when you feel tired, depleted, and wilting under the pressures of the world. By connecting with the lunar energy available, you fortify your own magic from the inside out to effortlessly work your light.

During the Full Moon, find a safe and private space. Outside is wonderful or near a window where you can see the moon. If this isn't possible, you can still imagine her light (it's always there).

Settle into the space. Light a fresh white candle and say:

> As this space is filled with light, I am filled with light.
> As the moon is full of light, I am full of light.
> I draw down your lunar fire to nourish every part of my being.
> With honor and reverence.

Mist the space with rose water or jasmine water (or any scent that feels good to you).

When you're ready, take a deep breath. Put yourself in a physical position that feels receptive. Find your center and focus on your breathing. Relax into the space around you and begin to feel the moonlight pouring over you. Feel it bathing you like soothing water.

Float in this feeling; drink it up with every part of your being. Let light enter every part of you, every cell, every cavern—deep into your soul. Just be in this moon bath. Your cells are literally transforming in this moonlight.

As the light pours in, your senses will tingle. Something in you will feel ignited. Like the moon, like the candle, you are glowing brightly. You have claimed your full expression and pulled moonlight into the lining of your skin.

Notice any impressions that come up while you're here. Just notice whatever the moonlight brings to the surface.

When you're ready, come back to the room and thank the moon for guiding and empowering you through your process. And know that she will always be there.

Let the candle burn out. Or relight it on each of the remaining days of the Full Moon.

• • •

There is no right or wrong way to draw down the moon. Always honor and trust your intuition with any ceremony. Simply looking at the moon when she is full and feeling her energy pouring over you can be your act of drawing down the moon.

You can begin any ceremony you perform during the Full Moon by drawing down the moon first.

An Elemental Ally: Crystal Talisman

Animism is the worldview that all things, both animate and inanimate, hold consciousness, Many shamanic traditions and tribal cultures see the world through this lens. They see and honor the special life force within everything, seeking to build right-relationship with the divine light within all things.

From this perspective, we can build connections that expand beyond the finite. We can connect with the presence and power of a tree. We can forge a powerful alliance with the energy of a body of water or a stone—anything.

This perspective is the foundation of crystal medicine. Each stone holds a special ally or elemental inside that you can connect with. Building a relationship with this special energy means they will offer their magic to you.

Quartz crystals are known to hold raw power and potential. These elementals draw and manifest desires that are impressed upon them. Simply speaking to them of your desire or dreams can help them build power and magnetism to manifest something into life.

To work with a quartz crystal elemental, simply:

- Hold the crystal in you hand, feeling the energy, warmth, and presence of this beautiful little being inside the crystal.

- Talk to the crystal; send loving thoughts and feelings to it.

- See what impressions show up for you. Look for a "connection" or a "click"—the deep knowing that you two are called to work together.

- When you get that sense of knowing, then begin to tell the crystal what you'd like help with. What would you like to have "crystallized" into life?

- See, feel, sense, or imagine this desire coming to life. And plant that seed into the crystal, asking the elemental within to help you with your desire.

- Express love and gratitude for the crystal's connection and assistance.

- Keep the crystal with you. Tuck it under your pillow. Place it in your pocket during the day. Sleep with it on your body. Keep it in your sacred space.

Take a moment each day to connect with your intention, the crystal's energy, and anything that shows up. Sometimes you'll get insight to honor the crystal energy in some way. This could be by placing it in the moonlight to soak up moon-juice, or running it under cold water, or passing it through some incense smoke, or offering it a bit of honey.

You can do this with all crystals. Trust your instinct as to which crystals you feel drawn to. These elemental beings can become lifelong allies for big magic.

Charging Objects in Moonlight

You can charge any sacred object in the light of the Full Moon. This will imbue the object with extra power.

Water is a wonderful element to charge with moonlight. This water can be added to moon baths, washes, sprays, or used to anoint your body or clothing. You can charge your oracle deck in moonlight to awaken and strengthen your connection.

Simply place the chosen object in a window where the moonlight flows in. Or you can put objects in large mason jars and place them outside where the light flows freely.

Make sure you gather your sacred objects before the sun rises.

Energetic Correspondences for the Full Moon

Here are some correspondences for the Full Moon phase to help you craft your own ceremonies and practices and to deepen your connection with tools you're already familiar with.

Stones and crystals:

- Selenite to raise the light body.

- Moonstone to connect with the Lunar Self.

- Girasol to connect with your truth.

Herbs, oils, and flower essences:

- Lavender for peace and patience, to trust the process.

- Patchouli because it draws in whatever you desire.

- Olive to ease exhaustion over effort.

- Mimulus to accept what you know.

Oracle cards:

- *Lunar Nomad Oracle*: Seer, Bouquet, Fish, Moon, and Book.

- Tarot: High Priestess, World, Star, and Judgment.

CHAPTER 10

Changing Faces, Changing Phases

You are brave, my wild-hearted friend. You dedicated yourself to the alchemical process of transformation. Stepping into the vast darkness all around you, you traversed the lands of shadow and light. Charting your journey by the moon's growth, you watched as she seeded the night sky with her splendor.

Day by day her majesty crowned the sky, growing fuller and brighter, and more expressed. Her journey has been a mirror of your own inner work. You've found a body of light wrapped in layers of shadow. Through this experience you committed the most radical, audacious act you can— becoming empowered!

This intimate connection with your inner magic isn't some fleeting thing. You've spun dreams into reality. You've felt the enchanted blood of your authentic nature coursing through you. Whatever gifts have been offered through this experience, they were all born from the womb of your own creative core.

The spell of light is now fading into the sky. Moving you back into the velvety hush of your inner world. Now is a time of rest, of release and regeneration. The light isn't gone; it's just retreated inward . . . to again go through the process of becoming. The waking dream isn't over; no, the dream has only begun.

You're Crowned in Light

There will come a time when you believe everything is finished; that will be the beginning.

—LOUIS L'AMOUR

If I can express anything to you, anything of value, it is that you are powerful. You are so powerful that it's surreal. I am in awe of how powerful we are. We are all such beautiful, creative, and vulnerable beings. Forged in the fire of experience and shaped by our own will, we get to create ourselves, express ourselves, and tell our stories.

Don't leave this experience wishing to banish all the pain and heartbreak in your life. Rather, see those experiences from a new perspective. They brought you to this moment in time, to the right place, asking the right questions, to receive the big answer—that you are destined to thrive. Don't forsake your past, don't long for your future. Let yourself be the space illuminated between them.

Where you are right now is absolutely perfect because there is no other place to be. Be moved by the experiences around you, let the tides of change and transformation wash over you and reveal that beautiful being that is cradled deep inside of you.

Everything you are, everything you've done, and everything you will do are powerful, worthy, and significant. No matter how lost you've felt, you've always been right here. You're never lost. And even when you thought you would split into a million pieces, completely broken by whatever happened, it was an evolution.

Let yourself glow and grow right here. Let yourself unfold magnificently. Exult yourself with the knowing that you're blessed with a creative force, a light, a magic that can never be taken from you, can never be lost, and will always pull you forward. The more you allow it, the greater the expression becomes. There is no limit to what you can do.

A Releasing Rite

Write a letter to anyone or anything you're still holding on to—past, present, or future. Write a letter of forgiveness and release. Set yourself free so you can reclaim your life, your power, and your purpose.

This letter can be simple or complex. Whatever you need to say, put it on the page. You could address each person or experience separately or all together. There is power in naming a thing. So name who or what you can, and that way you go straight to the root.

You might write:

> Dear (person who hurt me),
> I release you from the responsibility of my pain. I release you from my anger. I release you from my sadness. I release you from my fear. I release you from the weight and burden.
> I forgive you. I forgive you for everything. I release you and I forgive you.

And I thank you. I thank you for being a mirror. I thank you for playing in this experience. I thank you for being a manifestation of my light and shadow.

I thank you and I honor you for opening the door to a whole new life. I release you. I forgive you. I thank you. And I honor you.

I love you.

Write out your letter. Write with as much feeling and passion as you can muster. Let it all come to the surface. And then speak these words of release and forgiveness. Feel every part of you light up as you read those words. Express with every part of yourself, your voice, your body, and your heart. Let it all come through.

Then, with a match, set the letter on fire. Lay it in a fireproof bowl, and let it be consumed by the flames, until it is nothing but ash.

When the ashes are cool, take them outside under the Waning Moon and set them free. Toss your words into the night, into the wind, and into the cycle of release. Whatever you let go of will be recycled into the cosmic flow and turn into the clay of some new creation.

Creating the Luminous Body Ceremony

Phase by phase you've discovered so many facets of your being from your shadow to you light. Your past experiences, your fear, pain, and trauma are just aspects of you. There is still so much power and potential waiting to be discovered. Even when you feel limited or unable to stretch any wider, there are possibilities waiting to find you.

Creating the Luminous Body is a ceremony to help you see the enormity of your presence and power! Through this ceremony, you will experience a profound connection that will lead you to a creative discovery.

Gather your oracle deck and a large white cloth in front of your altar. You will want your journal to take notes and a way to photograph your layout. Take a moment for stillness and connect with your oracle cards.

When you feel ready, begin to shuffle your deck. Imagine yourself glowing with bright white light. See yourself as bright as the Full Moon. Your light begins to fill the deck to reveal your magic!

Set your intention by saying:

I am light. I am shadow.
I am a being of unlimited magic and potential.
Through these cards my luminous body is revealed.
So shall it be.

When you're ready, choose each card one by one for each of the lines below and lay them out in front of you in a straight vertical line. Imagine you are assembling a little person.

My crown of light.
My inner eyes.
My true voice.
My eternal heart.
My center of creation.
My sustaining roots.

Choose two more cards.

Lay one to the right for your Lunar Self:

My power to dream.

Lay one to the left for your Solar Self:

My power to build.

Imagine the cards before you are a luminous body with arms outstretched. Explore the images. Let the whole thing unfold before you. Notice what stands out to you. Let yourself be deeply moved by this experience.

Be aware of whatever is happening within you. Ask for a vision and let it come through. There's no need to judge or critique—just experience. Let your luminous body show you whatever needs to be seen.

Everything has a purpose here. If you feel drawn to a card or repelled by one, explore that a little deeper. Remember, you are the interplay of light and shadow—that's what makes you luminous.

Journaling the Lunar Journey

Take some time to journal on this spread. Ask yourself what you are being called to do next.

I encourage you to speak out loud to your luminous body.

In some way illustrate your luminous body!

You could draw something based on the impressions you saw in each image. You could create a crystal grid, choosing one crystal for each area. You could pick a color from each card, and light a candle for each body part. You could pick a key word for each body part, and write that word on that part of your body to really feel it settle in.

Take a photo to save and refer back to this whenever you'd like.

PART THREE

Lunar Magic
When You Need It

CHAPTER 11

When to Work Your Magic

Working through each phase of the moon is a powerful form of radical release, healing, and self-empowerment. You have experienced much personal growth along with your moon observances. But there is always more: you can always go deeper, higher, and wider.

You might notice a general sense of ease happening in your life. Maybe you've found more clarity about personal situations and experiences that have vexed you for years. Now that you have this insight, you can begin working more intently to transform your experience to reflect your deepest desires and honor your highest good.

I see the weekly moon practices as an overall observance of your personal growth and power. You could imagine this as a tidying up of your internal workspace, gathering all your supplies, setting the goal, and then diving into the more intricate work.

In this section you will find a number of magical practices organized by intention, desire, or condition. If you have a clear idea around what you want to change—whether it is bringing something new into your life, dealing with a situation already happening in your life, or getting rid of a situation—then you can look for a practice in this section to unify your inner desire with inspired action.

Always remember that what I share here is a framework. I encourage you, as the artist of your own life and magic, to tailor these practices to your own needs.

Practical magic is a supportive measure for your life and well-being. You have the power to work magic whenever you need it. Listen to your own inner call, when you feel drawn to work magic for change that will be the most potent time available.

However, you can amplify your magic by aligning it with the four phases of the moon that you've learned to work with. The phase of the moon doesn't dictate your personal ebb and flow; it only accommodates the vibration you already embody.

If you can align your spell work with the moon phase, that will be an added boost of power, but don't feel locked into a phase when you are in need. Magic is at your fingertips whenever you ask for it!

Magical Work by the Moon

The Waning Moon

Work magic to banish, decrease, or clear away the influence of something during the Waning Moon. Imagine, as the moonlight recedes from the night sky, the influences of your target waning with it. This is an especially potent time to banish debt, lose weight, break a habit, or expel doubt and fear. Perform spiritual cleansing, declutter, or focus on inner journey work. During the Waning Moon, you are decreasing the hold something has on you. Think of this as a time of clearing, letting go, making space, and opening yourself up for something better. You could work magic to banish an illness, a troublesome person, an abusive relationship, or anything you need to clear out of your life. Then you can plant a new seed of intention during the New Moon.

The New Moon

Work magic for new beginnings, to open doors, to set something in motion. At this time your spell work should aim to ready the space for something. Focus your intention on your inner state and how best to set the stage for a bigger desire. Work magic for self-love, to boost confidence, to renew your faith, to grow your enthusiasm, or to hone in on how you want to feel. During this moon, energies are still more malleable, so focus on kneading your desires into shape.

The Waxing Moon

Work magic under the Waxing Moon to increase something, to lay the foundation, and to get more specific. During the Waxing Moon, you can be more specific around your desire by moving from how you want to feel to what you want to experience. This is the time to call in new opportunities in all areas of your life from love and happiness to money and good health. The energy is ripe for creating and laying foundations. Work magic to strengthen connections or to bring harmony to a situation. You can perform magic aimed at protection, strengthening boundaries, or increasing support in some way. I always imagine this moon like the incubation stage—whatever you've mixed together, now goes in the oven to be transformed!

The Full Moon

Work magic aimed at quick results, to wrap things up, to reap the rewards, or to express gratitude. Full Moon energy is palpable; you can aim your magic at almost anything and get results. This makes it especially useful for emergency magic or when you need quick results. Keep in mind that magic can only do so much if you haven't made the space for the results to bloom. For example: You could work magic when you need money for rent, but that won't fix your overall financial situation. Because I see this phase as a threshold, I like to give thanks to my spirit helpers for any prior successes. Perform ceremonies of gratitude or to bring something to a positive close, such as a project, a final interview, a deal, and so forth. The Full Moon is very helpful for divination work, exploring the crystal ball, charging magical items, or increasing spiritual connection.

CHAPTER 12

The Power of Agreement and Ceremony

When your reality doesn't match your desire, there is a conflict of belief. Some part of you is not in *agreement* with that desire. When you experience a kink in your expression—whether in exercises, meditation, or ceremony—then you should explore it deeper to understand the roots, or the "disagreement."

- Alignment or full agreement feels like fluid motion, rhythm.

- Disturbance or disagreement feels like resistant, blocked motion, and hurdles.

Most of us see the world and ourselves in a very linear fashion. The idea of looking at life, experience, and reality from many different points of view is not readily accepted, especially when you're asked to see from your own unique lens. In part, this is because we've been robbed of our sense of choice and ownership, and we don't see the connection between inner state and outer experience.

But in every moment you're making an agreement, an energetic choice, that pulls everything into alignment. The question is: What are you aligning with? When you're in full agreement with your desire, then everything begins to move effortlessly. And, when static shows up on the line, it allows you to see where you're in disagreement so you can realign.

These energetic agreements happen:

- Mentally (consciously/unconsciously/subconsciously)—Air

- Physically (actions/responsibilities/choices)—Earth

- Emotionally (feelings/memories/dreams)—Water

- Spiritually (beliefs/practices/energetically)—Fire

For example: If you deeply desire money. You can consciously say, "I want lots of money." But you keep thinking thoughts and feeling feelings ("I am lacking") that agree with NOT having money. Then you have a disagreement, and your desire will not manifest clearly.

This is the reason we stay in draining relationships and experiences, because some part of us agrees with it and some other part of us doesn't, and so the kink forms. But you've found a secret: the secret powers of awareness and choice. Most of us just accept the way things are, and rather than digging deeper to see how we've allowed a situation, we point the finger at someone else.

Smart magic is done by taking ownership—you have no chance of fulfillment if you give your power away.

Ceremony is a powerful way to get into agreement or alignment with your desire. When you're working ceremony, you rouse your inner awareness, drawing to the surface some part of your consciousness that isn't always alert. You deliberately make the choice to show up, do the thing, and let it happen!

Ceremony is an energetic signal and a symbolic gesture that activates your inner magic by aligning the body, mind, emotions, and spirit. As you work ceremony, it eases the resistance around the desire and lets your expression unfold.

If you know some part of you is in disagreement or disharmony with your desire, then your ceremony can accommodate that particular aspect of yourself.

For example, you might do a spiritual cleansing bath when you feel your body is holding on to and resisting change. You might do a meditation when you feel your mind won't focus on your desire. You might do a journaling session when you need to get something off your chest before allowing the desire to come.

Prompts for Creating Magic

You can think of this as a formula, a way to *deliberately* create your magic. These aren't rules, just suggestions. And nothing about this has to be linear. Use this as a platform to assess your situation, and use your energetic story as a prompt for ceremony and practices that change the narrative.

- **Notice the experience.** What does your world look like? What feels good? What feels bad? What major thing are you facing? What are you tolerating?

- **Explore the energy.** Use the oracles + inner awareness to access the roots of your experience. Where does it come from? Why is it there? How is it serving you? What part of you wants this?

- **Notice the signs.** What stands out in the cards? What repeated omens keep appearing? What thought, feeling, memory, or sensation shows up? Is this mental, physical, emotional, or spiritual?

- **Work your light.** What action can you take now? What thought could you choose? What feeling would feel good? What words would nourish you?

- **The Four Elements.** Air (mental), water (emotional), earth (physical), fire (spiritual): What element might you choose to work with?

- **Create your own ceremony.** It doesn't have to be complex. Let spirit move you. You've learned many different ceremonies.

CHAPTER 13

Two Types of Magic

Before you choose a spell or ceremony, consider why you are working magic. I believe we are all meant to thrive, and, intrinsically, we are all whole. This is why I work magic from a holistic point of view. First, you want to be in full agreement with the desire you are working toward. In the previous chapter, I shared the concept of the power of agreement, and how you can desire something on one level and yet oppose it on another.

Following the ceremonies for each moon phase will help you get clearer on all levels, so that when you begin working spells for specific intentions, you've already achieved that state of agreement. But there's always more that can be done!

If you view magic as a way of bringing yourself into balance and harmony with the ebb and flow of life, then you'll have a clearer understanding of what you desire and why you are working a spell. You wouldn't work magic to draw a new lover to you if you know you're not ready for a relationship; in that instance you might want to work magic to clear cords and stuck feelings lingering from a past relationship.

Think about magic in two ways:

Banishing or Clearing Magic

Banishing magic is used to clear a situation or energy from your life. Think of this like pulling the weeds, cutting away the vines, and making the space for something new to be planted. You wouldn't start throwing seeds into a flower bed that is riddled with weeds and trash. Banishing magic can be used to clear away anything from a troublesome person, a painful memory or feeling, a precarious situation, or a debt.

Drawing or Attraction Magic

Drawing magic is worked to bring something into your life. Think of this magic like planting seeds in a well-tilled garden. You've made the space, cultivated the soil, and intently selected the plants you'd like to grow. Drawing magic can be used for anything from love, to money, or a new home. When you draw something to you, be sure that you're ready to receive it.

If you're new to working magic, you might feel ready to dive in and work spells for all the things you want in your life, all the things that are missing. But you have to ask: Why? Why are they missing in the first place? Usually there is something that needs to be cleared before you can draw in the thing you really desire.

Often I suggest banishing magic first to make the space for something better to show up. Many times I find when we work through the baggage and banish the blocks, the thing we desired comes naturally, without having to work magic for it! But sometimes those things can use a boost or extra encouragement.

For example: Do you want to draw money to pay a debt? Well, then work magic to banish you debt, rather than draw money.

• • •

In the following chapter, you'll discover a variety of spells to transform your life. Whenever you are in need of change, browse through this section and identify a spell that aligns with your need, desire, or intention.

For each spell, I have identified the moon phase that best aligns with the intention of the spell. However, magic can be worked whenever you need it. Your internal phase is just as potent as the astronomical phase of the moon. Keep this in mind: the moon doesn't dictate the spell; it only amplifies the energies you raise and project out into the Universe.

I have written these spells to help you in times of need, and to hopefully inspire you to create your own magic. Use them in their entirety or as a basis for a more personalized work. I believe magic is art—allow yourself to be creative!

CHAPTER 14

Spells by Intention, Need, or Desire

The most powerful magic you can perform is making a choice! Choose to do something about your life, take your destiny into your own hands, and know that you deserve to thrive!

When Struggling with Uneasy Feelings

Moon phase: Waning Moon, Any Phase

Perform this spell when you need to let go of uneasy feelings about a person or situation. This is especially helpful when you cannot stop thinking about something or you need to shift your mood. The Waning Moon will amplify the release of energy you will experience with this spell, but this will be beneficial whenever you need it.

This spell is done by going for a walk in nature to a body of water. I like to do this in the evening when the air feels cool and the world starts to wind down. Usually I wear something of a darker color that is flowing and comfortable, to align with my desire for freedom and surrender, but you should wear whatever feels comfortable.

Choose the body of water you will walk to. If you need to drive to the location, that is perfectly fine, but give yourself a little time to walk to the water and explore. As you ready yourself for this journey, let all the feelings bottled up inside come to the surface. Let all the thoughts and feelings flood your awareness and move through you. Feel the energy moving through you body, all your limbs, circulating through every vein.

As you walk, feel the energy moving through you and into the ground. Whatever you can let go of, let it go at this moment, but there's no need to rush. Make your way to the body of water. Know that this will be a cool, calm place of reprieve. Along the way, keep your eyes out for something to hold—a small stone or stick is best.

When you have made your way to the body of water, sit there for a few minutes. With your natural token in hand, hold it tightly and imbue it with all the uneasy feelings that still linger in your system. Push everything into this stick or stone—imagine that it is like a sponge, absorbing it all.

Sometimes I will speak out loud as I do this. Try talking out all the things you're thinking and feeling. Confide in the wind, the water, and this natural token. Get it off your chest, cry, be angry—don't censor yourself.

When you are ready to part with these feelings, toss the object into the water. Feel the release that comes from letting it go, into the water, back to nature, back to the Universe.

Say this prayer:

I surrender these heavy feelings.
I surrender my torment and pain.

I surrender my attachment to this situation.
I give it to the great forces of nature . . . wash it away.
Set me free so I can live, thrive, and be.
With gratitude and respect.
So shall it be.

Easing Fatigue and Nourishing Yourself

Moon phase: New Moon

When you feel physically tired and drained, your energy can seem low, making it hard to get traction for goals and desires. The beginning of a New Moon is a great time to perform this bath ceremony to ease fatigue, nourish your body, and amplify your energy. This will help you recharge after the heavy, inward facing vibrations of the Waning phase.

Set aside some special time to treat yourself to a respite, and recharge your reserves. Slipping into the cocoon of a warm bath is one of my favorite rituals. This ceremony calls on the power of basil and sweet almond oil to charge the bath, uplift the spirit, and soothe your tired body.

Sweet Almond and Basil

Sweet almond oil is one of the best oils for the skin and hair. It is highly absorbent, light, and hypoallergenic. It is filled with vitamins and minerals and has a high content of proteins and vitamin E. It soothes the skin and leaves it feeling loved and refreshed.

Energetically, sweet almond oil infuses you with self-love and much needed nourishment. It pulls in positive vibrations to soothe, support, and sustain you. And it amplifies your magnetism to positive opportunities and favorable influences.

Basil is an old herb used for love, prosperity, and protection. It has been said that wherever basil is planted, evil cannot enter. Adding a dash of basil to your food integrates love and radiance into your aura. Adding it to your bath will eradicate negative influence, filling your aura with light and intention to attract only good vibrations.

STEP 1. PREPARING FOR MAGICAL CEREMONY

Perform this ceremony after a long day. In the evening retreat from the world, turn off your phone, and forget about your concerns.

Gather the following:

A few sprigs of fresh basil

A bottle of sweet almond oil

A fresh white candle

A clean white towel to dry off with

- You've gathered your accoutrements, and you are ready to create sacred space. Begin by running a bath of warm water. Make sure the water is to your liking so that you can rest and relax in the embrace of the tub. This is a meditative experience, a form of silent prayer.

- Hold the sprigs of basil between your hands. Begin to massage and bruise the sprigs and leaves to release aromatic oils. Ask for basil's potent spirit to fill your bath with energy. As the scent fills the air, let it invigorate your senses and uplift your energy. Now hold the bruised springs under the faucet as the tub fills in order to disperse the oils, and then toss the sprigs in the bath.

- Now pour some sweet almond oil into your palms. Take a moment to feel the nourishing power of this oil and ask the spirit of this oil to bless you. Place your palms under the faucet again, and allow the oil to slip through your fingers into the warm water.

STEP 2. IGNITING INTENTIONS

Before you slip into this restorative bath, rub the remaining oil from your palms onto the fresh white candle. As the oil warms between your palms, fill it with your intention to ease your fatigue and fill you with good energy. If you have specific needs for self-care, then name them at this time For example: easy sleep, time to yourself, etc.

- Light the candle. Set it where you can gaze at it softly during your bath.

- Gently slip into the tub. Let the water wash over you. Soak in the warm embrace of the water. Cup water in your palms and rub it over your body, your neck, the base of your head, into your scalp and feet. Be kind to yourself in this bath.

- All the while gaze over at the flame, remembering your intention. Close your eyes and let the flame dance in your mind, let the warmth of the tub lull you deeper, and the scent carry you into trance.

- Be here with your intention. Surrender to the soothing energy of the this space. See yourself filled up until every fiber of your being glows and hums with feelings of love, peace, and positivity.

- When you've finished, end with a prayer of thanks to the Universe, your Spirit Circle, and the botanicals used. Towel dry. Let your candle burn. And relax for the remainder of the evening.

Know that good magic fills and surrounds you now!

Repeat this ceremony as often as you like. Use it when you work with the New Moon or when you are starting a new project. Or use it to unwind after a long week, a stressful project, or whenever your spirit needs a little TLC. This is an especially beneficial bath during the long winter months.

Compost the sprigs of basil after your bath, thanking them for their help, and thank Mother Nature for her regenerative power.

Breaking Bonds with a Negative Experience

Moon phase: Waning Moon

Nettle is a wonderful plant spirit to purge negative energetic attachments with people or situations. Nettle can banish limiting thoughts, emotional patterns, and psychic cords. These psychic cords can be deliberate psychic intrusions or stray energies collected through daily living. Or they may be a connection to a specific person, experience, or situation you still have ties to—physically or emotionally.

When I find myself enmeshed in a web of negative energy, I like to use nettle to clear the slate and help me find my center. Nettle can even help when dealing with emotional pain from bad habits, obsessive thoughts, and emotional baggage.

Remember that removing negative or misaligned energy from your life is only half the process. You must create a firm practice that keeps the energy from returning.

Nettle often purges toxic energies and helps you gain a moment of clarity to see how to implement a better course of action. Have a clear intention that, by purging these attachments, you are gaining composure, adding empowerment to own your personal energy, and creating situations more conducive to your well-being.

Work with the spirit of nettle during a Waning Moon.

NETTLE TEA

Brew a strong cup of nettle tea to help eliminate stuck feelings and energies rooted in your energy body. As the tincture steeps, ask the helpful spirit of nettle to untie the bonds between you and the situation. Be as specific as you can, naming out loud into the steam whatever you wish to have undone.

When the tea is cool enough to drink, focus on the expulsion of these influences from your life. Let the warm tea move through your body, as you feel all the attachments being undone, releasing your head and heart from their heavy hold. Imagine what you will do with this new energetic space that has been freed up.

I like to add peppermint to my nettle tea for a more pleasant flavor. Peppermint purges negative energy and brings about a clearer state of being. Use this clear headspace for dreaming up positive actions.

Enjoy a cup of nettle tea each night of the Waning Moon to dispel especially trying situations.

WASHING WITH NETTLE

Washing with nettle tea yields similar results to drinking it. A nettle bath tends to work a bit faster if you are dealing with more aggressive situations. I prefer this practice if I am dealing with something extremely heavy, especially if I have some awareness that the source is outside of myself.

Make a strong cup of nettle tea as if you were drinking it. Then add the tea to pitcher of warm water. Add a handful of sea salt to amplify the cleansing power of the bath. Always ask for the spirit of the botanicals or minerals to lend their power to your ceremony.

Take your pitcher to the bathroom where you will have plenty of privacy. Sitting in an empty bathtub slowly pour the pitcher of tea over your head (please make sure the tea has sufficiently cooled to no hotter than lukewarm). Envision the water flushing away the energy of whatever has had a hold on you.

As you pour the water over your head, brush your body with your hands in downward strokes. From your crown, to your neck, torso, arms, middle section, down to your legs and feet. Imagine all the energetic debris being sloughed off.

Add a prayer or affirmation while you perform this cleansing ceremony. Speak from the heart; use the prayer below or something similar:

With this wash I am released from the hold of (name the situation).
I am free of these bonds.
Now my light can shine.
So shall it be!

NETTLE POWDER

Grind nettle leaves or open a preground packet of nettle tea. Sprinkle the powder over a self-igniting coal. As the smoke rises around you, speak out loud the things you wish to be free from. Ask the spirit of nettle to help remove the ties that bind you.

You can clear your home in the same manner. Open the windows and walk throughout your house while burning nettle powder on a coal. Always start in the back of your house, and make your way to the front door. Speak out loud the things you wish to free yourself from.

To Lift Your Spirit When You Don't Feel Good Enough

Moon phase: Full or Waning Moon

Magic can enhance your mood when you feel depressed with heavy feelings like grief, sadness, or self-doubt. You can perform this magic when the moon is full or waning or whenever you are in need. Always work magic of this nature along with the proper medical and psychological help—magic is a support, not a solution.

Frankincense has long been regarded as a sacred resin. It was one of the three gifts of the Magi, and many traditions have burned frankincense to carry prayers to the divine, to ask for blessings, or as a sign of respect to invisible forces.

The scent of frankincense is clean, sweet with slight citrus or pine notes. Burning frankincense tears or diffusing the oil has a clearing effect that cuts through mental clutter, disentangles feelings, and offers a sense of gentle release. It's been known to lift depression and enhance positive feelings.

When you sense heavy feelings settling around you, find a safe and private space to diffuse a bit of frankincense oil. Add a few drops to your palms and breathe in the scent. Feel it work through your body, untangling the knots of tension and anxiety. Keep breathing into this feeling of surrender and begin to rub your palms vigorously together.

Hold your hands out with palms faced upward. Begin to see, sense, or feel warm light flow into your palms. Imagine gathering it up like a soothing balm.

Now place your palms on the crown of your head and begin rubbing downward as if you are sweeping over your whole body with this balm. Brush down the length of your body, your arms, your trunk, your legs, and feet. Spend extra time on any part of your body that feels in need.

As you do this say:

Lift this heavy cloud.
Fill me with light.
Bless my body with strength.
Bless my mind with clarity.

Bless my heart with peace.
Bless my spirit with healing.
I am enough.
So shall it be.

When you are finished, rest for as long as you can.

This ritual can boost your spirit during a turbulent times or before going into a trying situation. I find it's also helpful before performing difficult or focused tasks such as studying.

A Circle of Protection for Your Home

Moon phase: Waxing or Full Moon; or Any Phase

Circles have a long history of magical uses. As an unbroken, continuous figure, the circle represents unity, completion, cycles, and boundaries. Used as a sigil, a circle can become a container or boundary for safekeeping.

A protective circle can be placed around buildings, objects, and people. Anything stationary can be easily placed in a circle.

When you create a circle of protection, it becomes an energetic barrier holding unwelcomed things at bay. When placed on the ground, the center becomes consecrated space, called a magic circle. This is a place where many magical workers will perform their ceremonies.

However, you can create a protective circle whenever you are in need of a sanctuary from forces known or unknown. A protective circle is particularly valuable when you feel psychically weak, emotionally drained, or sense the influence of some oppressive energetic force. A protective circle can be used to shield you or your home from physical harm if there are no immediate signs of danger.

Cornmeal can be used to create a protective boundary around your home. Gather cornmeal in a bowl and stand at your front door, holding the bowl in both hands. Take a moment to set your intention by relaxing, grounding yourself in this moment, and saying:

> With this cornmeal I draw a boundary of protection from all
> harm seen and unseen, known and unknown.
> Protect my home, myself, and all those welcomed within.
> No harm shall cross this boundary; only benevolent forces
> are welcomed within.
> So shall it be.

Now drizzle a thin line of cornmeal around the perimeter of your home, starting at the front door and moving clockwise until you return to the place you started. As you draw this circle, envision the line as a violet light encircling the space. Know that this is a boundary of protection from all harm.

If you live in an apartment and are unable to place a circle of protection around the outside of your space, you can create a circle on the inside of your unit. Rather than using cornmeal, you will employ four clear quartz crystals.

Wash these crystals in spring water. Then begin at the front door, holding the crystals in both palms. As described above, set your intention to create a protective boundary. Ask the spirits of the crystals for their aid in creating this energetic barrier. Repeat the above incantation.

Now place a crystal at the front door. Walking clockwise, place a one crystal at the right side of the home. Place a crystal in the back of the home. Place a crystal at the left side of the home. As you place each crystal, imagine a violet line connecting one crystal to the next, until you arrive back to the front door. Envision the space being sealed in this protective barrier.

You can create a circle using the same method around a room, your bed, or your work area. This protective circle is temporary. Reform your circle at each Waxing or Full Moon. If you notice the boundary has been tampered with, take it as a sign that the circle has absorbed an energetic blow, and recreate the circle using the above method.

To Be Worn for Protection from Harmful Influences

Moon phase: Full Moon

You can craft a simple amulet to protect yourself from harmful influences, such as intrusive energies from strangers during your daily routine, to avert the attention of negative people, to ward off troublesome thoughts, or to keep nightmares and restless sleep at bay.

This amulet is very helpful if you work in a high-stress environment, if you deal with strangers regularly, or if you take public transportation. You can also place this amulet on loved ones, such as children, if you feel they need extra protection.

Craft this amulet on the Full Moon. Gather a 12-inch length of red cord or ribbon, dried basil, a self-igniting coal, a firesafe container, and a lighter.

In a safe space that is well ventilated, gather your supplies. You can perform this work on your altar if you keep one, or simply reserve a special tray on which to place your items.

Begin by taking a few minutes for stillness and to connect with your breath. Now light the self-igniting coal in the firesafe container, and blow on the coal until it fully ignites and glows orange-red. With your intention in mind, begin to sprinkle the dried basil on the coal until it forms a nice plume of smoke, while saying:

Spirit of basil, I ask for your protection.
Protection from harm seen and unseen, known and unknown.
So shall it be.

Holding the length of ribbon in your hands, pass it through the smoke, while saying:

I now make this ribbon an amulet of protection.
Protect me (or the person it is for) from harm seen and unseen,
        known and unknown.
So shall it be.

If this amulet is for you to wear, tie it around your ankle or wrist, wrapping it around three (or a multiple of three) times, and tying it with three knots. Say:

This ribbon is an amulet of protection.

Protect me (or the person it is for) from harm seen and unseen,
known and unknown.
So shall it be.

Take a moment to feel the amulet imbuing you with an aura of safety.

At this time, the basil should have burned completely (there is no need to add more).

If you've fashioned this amulet for another person, wrap it in a piece of white cloth until you can give it to them. Follow the same instructions above for tying the amulet on them. You can simply hold your intention in mind as you tie the amulet to the person if you're uncomfortable repeating it out loud.

When the ribbon breaks, you can fashion a new amulet.

Alternately, you can perform the above spell with a whole spool of red thread, and stitch a small circle as a protective amulet inside your clothing or the clothing of family members.

A Crystal Bath When You Feel Sensitive

Moon phase: Any Phase

Empaths are highly attuned, sensitive individuals who have a natural connection to the subtle worlds. These are the subtle worlds of thought, emotion, spirit, and energy. These people tend to be artistic, intuitive, and right-brained individuals who process the world around them through feeling and intuition.

It is essential for empathic people to take time for rest and relaxation. This is how you disconnect from harmful energies and recharge yourself so that you feel more vital. I urge you to make a daily ritual of this. You will find yourself improving every day.

A powerful way to recharge your essence and bring yourself to center is through the ritual of bathing. Bathing has been a powerful form of energetic cleansing for thousands of years, and it offers you a chance to charge your energy with good intention.

Adding crystals to your bathwater will create a unique vibration that can infuse the aura and invigorate the spirit. I have created a simple bath for empaths or when you feel sensitive.

CRYSTAL BATH FOR EMPATHS

Gather three crystals: citrine, amethyst, and rose quartz.

Citrine is the path opener stone. It pushes out negative vibrations and enhances the aura to a state of well-being. Amethyst is a stone of protection and clarity, opening the third eye to help with clear intuitive perception. Rose quartz is a heart stone, releasing any bound-up energies that may be clogging the heart center.

Combined together, these three stones create a calming, healing, and stabilizing vibration that will benefit anyone, especially the empath.

Also, gather essential oils of lavender, rosemary, and sage.

Lavender infuses the aura with peace, relaxation, and protection. It is very soothing to anxious nerves or heavy feelings. Rosemary infuses the aura with clarity and protection. The scent has a way of clearing your head from mind chatter. Sage infuses the aura with wisdom and discernment, and clears away negativity.

To create your sacred bath, fill your tub half full with warm water. Make sure that the temperature suits a relaxing state of mind. This is a type of meditation and isn't meant for cleaning your physical self. You are creating a sacred moment.

Add to the water three to five drops of each oil. Be sure to do this as the water runs, inserting the drops under the spout so that the oils are dispersed evenly throughout the bath.

Now place each stone into the water, focusing on their specific vibration. Ask for their energies to infuse the bath so that they may charge your aura to bring you into equilibrium and honor your highest good.

When the bath is ready, simply step in and sink down. Let yourself melt into the calming presence of the scents of the botanicals, the vibration of the crystals, and the serenity of being alone and in the moment.

Release anything that seems to be troubling you. Imagine that it is flowing out, into the water, and transformed by the water's healing properties. Let yourself be filled with light and vitality. Feel this in every fiber of your being. You are glowing.

Set an intention for yourself. Affirm that you are safe, balanced, and whole. Affirm that you are in this moment, now, fully present, open to the shift, and completely deserving of this gift.

Stay there for at least fifteen minutes. When you are finished, express a feeling of gratitude. Towel yourself dry, and turn in for the evening.

You can gather the crystals from the bath and sleep with them under your pillow or keep them in a silk pouch. Hold them near when you need their special energy medicine.

To Unbind Yourself from a Difficult Person

Moon phase: Waning Moon

If you feel trapped or bound to a person who just won't leave you alone, this spell will help cut the energetic cords that bind you. This is particularly helpful after a relationship has ended, but the person is still holding on. Situations like divorce, abusive relationships, stalkers, or toxic familial ties are ideally in need of this work.

Do not perform this spell lightly; you are severing the energetic ties that hold you to this person, so be very clear that you wish to have them gone.

Perform this spell on the Waning Moon. Gather together a photo of you and the person you are cutting ties with, a spool of black thread, a pair of scissors, a fireproof bowl, and a lighter.

With your tools gathered in your sacred space, begin with a moment of stillness and silence. Focus on your breathing, relax into this moment, and clearly hold your intention in mind.

Now take the photo of you and the other person and place them face together. If you have a photo of the two of you together, tear the photo down the center, then place the two pieces facing together.

Begin to wrap the black thread around both photos, binding them together. Wrap the photos three times around, cut any leftover length of thread away, and tie the bound photos with three knots.

Holding the bound photos in your hand, feel all the pain, fear, negativity, and emotion that have come from this toxic connection. As these feelings surge through you, say:

Constricting bonds that hold us tight.
Tied together in endless night.
They choke my breath.
They obscure my light.

Now take the scissors in one hand, while holding the wrapped photos in the other, and begin cutting the thread that binds you while you say:

I cut the cord.
I sever the tie.
I unbind the hold.
I set us free.
Go away . . . leave me be.
Without harm I work this charm.

When you've finished cutting the cords and repeating the charm, take the thread and the photo of the other person and burn them in the fireproof bowl. While they burn, say:

I burn the cord.
I burn the tie.
I release the hold.
I set us free.
Go away . . . leave me be.
Without harm I work this charm.

Let the remains of the photo and thread burn to ash. Discard the ashes somewhere away from your home. You can cast them into a body of water or leave them at the base of a friendly tree.

Take the photo of you and place it somewhere special. Place a rose quartz crystal for heart-mending energy next to it, or surround it with fresh flowers as a reminder of your freedom and your new life.

When You Need Money Quickly

Moon phase: Waning or Full Moon; or Any Phase

Use this spell when you need an extra boost of abundance or when you need money quickly for an expense. Work this spell during the Waning or Full Moon for added power. Remember, quick magic is a temporary fix, and you should always perform more in-depth work to help heal and resolve the underlying issues.

For this spell you will need a candle, honey, and the following herbs and spices: allspice, nutmeg, ginger, cloves, and basil.

If you have seven days to perform this spell, use a larger candle, if this is emergency magic, then use a small taper or chime candle.

You can also use "Pumpkin Pie Spice," which is usually a combination of allspice, nutmeg, ginger, and cloves. All of these spices have a fiery energy to get results and attract abundance quickly.

Basil is for banishing negative vibrations and generating good energy.

Honey is for creating sticky, sweet, attraction energy!

Hold your candle in both hands, filling it with feelings of abundance and prosperity. See, sense, and know with all your might that what you desire is coming to you. Let your whole body vibrate with this powerful affirmation.

Roll the candle in honey, or drizzle it with honey. Honey will add a layer of attraction to your candle work and help the spices stick to your candle. You don't need a lot of honey, just a nice thin layer.

Now sprinkle the spices and basil on the candle.

With each step keep your intention clear in your mind, while saying:

I attract what I desire with complete ease. All doors are open. All paths are clear. My blessings find me in unimaginable ways. I am magnetized with positive vibration. So shall it be.

After covering the candle with the herbs and spices you can light the wick and say:

I activate my inner magnetism to attract (x amount of money needed). This or something better comes to me in infinite and empowering ways, now!

Without harm, so shall it be.

Let the candle burn down, and then get out of the way and let the money come in!

If you are working this candle spell for seven days, then light the wick each day and let it burn for 15 to 20 minutes. Thank the candle each time you extinguish it. And repeat the words above before relighting.

Remember, you do not have to imagine/figure out/speculate on where the money will come from and how it will get to you or if it needs to be cash money at all! The creative unknown of the Universe will figure it out.

This is just one way to manifest an intention. It's only as powerful as you allow it to be. The spices hold vibrations that mingle with your own desire to bring about change, but your allowance of that change is the key.

Spiritual Cleansing and Blessing for the Home

Moon phase: Any Phase

Everyday tasks can turn into sacred acts with intention and forethought. One beneficial practice to your overall well-being is to energetically cleanse and bless your home as you do your regular cleaning routine. Your home is a reflection of your inner world, and an extension of your personal power, so when you fill your space with high vibrations, you can change all areas of your life.

Our ancestors understood that the home marked the intersection of the mundane and mystical and often incorporated magical elements in their everyday tasks. Much of the daily chores you perform—such as sweeping, mopping, dusting, and doing laundry—can become magically charged practices.

A simple way to turn these common chores into magical practices is setting the intention that you are clearing away dirt, dust, and stagnant energy. Having that clear vision in your mind will shift the overall vibration of your space. From there, you can play with different practices and cleaning products to amplify this intention.

One way I like to shift energy in my home is through washing. You can turn your cleaning bucket into a magical brew by adding natural ingredients for their energetic qualities. Lemon, vinegar, and pine all have been used to clean dirty homes for ages, and it's no coincidence that they're also very powerful for clearing away stuck energies.

Add some fresh squeezed lemon juice and vinegar to a bucket of water. Hold both hands over the bucket, filling it with positive energy and intention. Ask that this be a spiritual wash to remove all negative energy and influences. See, sense, and know that this wash now has the power to remove tough stains, dirt, and psychic debris from your home.

Then go about washing your space as you normally would. Use this water to wash your floors, counters, windows, doors, and anything else that can handle being wet-washed with a clean cloth. Pay special attention to doors! Then, when you're finished using this wash, pour the remaining water down the toilet and flush away those icky energies.

You can also add essential oils to your water, such as lemon, pine, sage, or Four Thieves Oil (a traditional blend of oils). These same ingredients can be used to create a spiritual cleansing bath for yourself after a long day of housework.

Infuse other tasks with intention. Dust rooms with a feather duster that has been blessed with the intention to clear away dust and energetic debris. Open windows to let out trapped energy in your space. Shake out rugs and draperies to break up stagnant energy. Launder your linens (especially your bed linens) with a bit of lemon juice or Florida Water (a powerful spiritual cologne) in the wash to remove lingering energies.

Sweeping has a long history in magic. An old folk tradition is to sprinkle a handful of salt on the floor after troublesome people have left your home, and then sweep the salt out the door and send their vibes away with them. You can use sweeping as a form of energy clearing by setting the intention, sprinkling salt throughout the house where you will be sweeping, and then, starting in the room farthest from your front door, sweep up all the dirt, dust, and salt along with the stray energy left behind. Discard in the trash as usual, but then you should take the trash out immediately—don't leave those energies sitting around to seep out.

You can vacuum with the same intention. You can trade the salt for baking soda. Just sprinkle around your carpets and let sit for 10 to 30 minutes, and then vacuum your space as usual. Remember to get rid of the debris afterward.

It's ideal to dust, sweep, and then wash the space in that order. It keeps everything nice and fluid. Washing gets rid of the last traces of energy that might be tossed around from your other chores.

You can finish your cleaning and cleansing by ringing a bell, or use a rattle throughout the house a few times to clear and bless the space. I like to go throughout the house with a special rattle I had made for me by a healer. As I go through the house, filling it with sound and vibration, I speak affirmations of blessing over the home. You can speak from the heart about whatever you want to fill the space with: love, happiness, good health, and prosperity.

If you are dealing with something difficult in your life, such as a conflict with your partner, financial troubles, or illness, you can shift the vibration by using these techniques. Oftentimes, cleaning your home, redecorating, or decluttering can expedite the healing process when nothing else seems to work.

I have one last practice I want to share, and this is my favorite: spiritual door washing to infuse your life with blessings. Think of your home as a metaphor for your entire life (it puts things into perspective doesn't it?), and imagine that your front door is the entranceway for all your opportunities. In that case, you want your door to invite in the good and keep out the bad.

First wash your front door with a cleansing wash like the one above. Wash it inside and out, from top to bottom. I live in an apartment building so I wash the paneling around my door and the walls on either side in the hallway.

After cleansing and cleaning the door with a lemon/vinegar wash, I do a second washing of the door to draw in positive influences. You can create a wash with rose water and orange blossom water to bring in love, healing, and prosperity. You can make a wash with Florida Water because it raises all vibrations and invites positive influences (it also smells divine). Or you can make a simple wash from a bag of Constant Comment tea, which is made from fruits and spices that are especially beneficial for healing, abundance, and blessings.

Rather than flushing away the remaining water from your second wash, pour the water across the threshold to your home to keep inviting good energy inside.

I end my door washing by lighting a stick of incense and offering it to the benevolent spirits of the land, the building, and those around me in spirit. I ask for their continued blessings and support, and I thank them for all they do. I then leave the incense to burn near the door entrance.

Even the seemingly mundane can be filled with magic! When you incorporate these practices into your daily chores, you fill your home and your life with deep intention. Every act becomes sacred work that supports your overall well-being.

To Open Your Psychic Senses

Moon phase: Full or Waning Moon

Brew a cup of dandelion root tea during the Full or Waning Moon to gently open your psychic senses. As you breathe in the steam, imagine your psychic sense tingling awake. Feel the power of the dandelion root encouraging your energy to be grounded, centered, and open to spiritual messages.

Drinking a cup of dandelion root tea before meditation or divination practices will sharpen your senses so you can perceive insights more clearly. Pass your oracle deck through the steam of your tea to further establish and strengthen the connection.

If you wish to connect with your spirit guides or someone in spirit, speak their name out loud into the steam. Doing this will welcome their presence and draw them near. As you sip your tea, allow yourself to slip into a light trance and notice if any messages or impressions come through.

Whenever you work with spirit helpers, always thank them for their time, insight, and energy. Then bid them farewell.

Lunar Alchemy

To Settle Restless Sleep or Nighttime Psychic Intrusions

Moon phase: Full and Waning Moon; or Any Phase

The times right before sleep, while we are sleeping, and right when we wake up are very active times for psychic or spiritual encounters because the analytical mind isn't as active, so intuitive impressions can slip through with ease. If you are extremely sensitive like myself, this could wreak havoc on your beauty sleep!

My whole life, I have had vivid dreams, often connected to psychic or spiritual experiences. I often receive visitations from people in spirit, get psychic impressions of events happening in some other place, have prophetic dreams, or experience astral projection. Sometimes these dreamtime experiences are peaceful and welcomed; other times they can be unsettling. I find that the Full and Waning Moon tend to increase this activity.

To help settle your disrupted sleep during these psychic episodes, try placing a piece of selenite on your bedside table or under your pillow. Selenite is a wonderful stone for raising vibration, creating an atmosphere of peace, joy, and tranquility. I find it works well to stave off nightmares or unsettling dreamtime encounters, which makes it great for young children.

If you feel unsafe while you sleep because of psychic intrusions, place a piece of black tourmaline next to your bed along with the selenite. Black tourmaline is my go-to protective stone. It seems to create an energetic stronghold that is especially useful during sleep.

You can take this a step further by placing a piece of black tourmaline at each corner of your bed, and a large piece of selenite at the head of your bed. Placing them under your bed where they will not be moved or disturbed is ideal. You can also get creative and incorporate the stones into your decor!

A DREAM PILLOW FOR PEACEFUL SLEEP

You are more sensitive to energies and impressions while you sleep, so setting a clear intention before bed is good practice. Meditation before bed, anointing yourself with special oils, and repeating affirmations are simple steps you can add to your nighttime ritual. I often tuck crystals, herbal sachets, or oracle cards under my pillow to align with a particular desire or intention. Check the correspondences in each moon phase chapter for ideas.

Creating a dream pillow is another beautiful way to encourage restful sleep, help you recall your dreams, and create a positive connection to your inner world. Dream pillows are simple and versatile magic, but here is a simple one to try for yourself.

For your dream pillow you will need a five- by seven-inch muslin bag, dried rosemary, lavender, chamomile, rose petals, jasmine flowers, hops, a stick of incense, and a silver marker.

Gather your tools and ingredients in a sacred space. Take some time for stillness and connect with your energy in whatever way feels right. When you are ready, light your incense. Now pass your ingredients through the smoke to bless and fill them with your desire for peaceful sleep, while saying:

With this smoke I conjure peaceful sleep.
With the aid of my spirit helpers.
So shall it be.

With the silver marker write the following on the outside of your muslin bag:

While I sleep, I have peaceful dreams.

Open the mouth of the bag so you can easily add each botanical one by one. (You can place the bag inside a small cup and fold the opening around the rim of the cup to keep it open.) Hold each herb in your hand, connecting with its essence, and ask for its aid in constructing this dream pillow.

As you do so repeat the following:

Rosemary helps me recall my dreams.
Lavender eases my active mind.
Chamomile attracts only positive dreams.
Rose petals bring loving energy.
Jasmine keeps my vision keen.
Hops lulls me deep to sleep.
While I sleep, I have peaceful dreams.
So shall it be.

After you've added each herb, breathe into the bag three times to imbue it with energy. Pull the drawstring to seal it tightly, wrapping the drawstring around the top to form a little bulge (to keep herbs from falling out), and knot it with three knots.

Place your dream pillow into the pillowcase of the pillow you sleep on. Before you drift off to sleep each night, repeat your intention to experience peaceful sleep.

If you need guidance, answers, or clarity about something at the start of the Full Moon, write your question on a small slip of paper, tuck it into another muslin bag along with your dream pillow, and place it back into your pillowcase. Pay close attention to your dreams during this moon phase to see what answers come through.

When you have your answers or when the moon phase changes, remove your slip of paper, and return your dream pillow to your pillowcase.

To Ease Vulnerability and Boost Self-Esteem

Moon phase: New Moon

It is human nature to feel vulnerable at some point or another. Traumatic situations can leave you feeling scattered and doubting yourself. Sometimes a harsh comment can drain you of all confidence. Maybe you've always felt a bit insecure about a personal attribute, and you're looking for a way to heal those icky feelings. This spell will help you conjure good self-esteem when you need it most and remind you that you are a beautiful, precious gift to the world.

Perform this spell during the New Moon. For this spell you are creating a spell jar that you can use over and over again. I find spell jars are very effective for ongoing work. The idea is simple: once you construct the jar, you will shake it up whenever you need a boost of good self-esteem energy.

Gather together a clear glass jar with a lid, a photo of yourself small enough to fit inside of the jar, silver and gold glitter, a piece of tumbled carnelian, an ink pen, and the following herbs: rose petals, calendula, angelica, hyssop, and a bay leaf.

Give yourself time to create your spell jar and find a private space. Take some time to become still and relaxed. Turn your awareness to the insecurities or vulnerabilities you're feeling. Notice what triggers those feelings. Is there a person or situation tied to these feelings? Is it something about yourself? How would you like to feel?

The intention of this spell isn't to change anything about yourself. Rather, this magic will conjure from deep within you the confidence and awareness that you are enough as you are. By working this spell you are encouraging a change in your perspective so you can see, feel, and know how wonderful you are.

On the back of your photo, write a positive affirmative statement that embodies how you want to feel. Write this statement as if it is already a reality, because it is on a deeper level.

You could write something like this:

I love my body for protecting me and allowing me to experience this beautiful life.

When you've written a clear statement that feels right, read it out loud to yourself a few times. Feel your vibration shifting. Feel yourself becoming light, stronger, more empowered.

After immersing yourself in those feelings kiss your photo. Then place it in the jar so you can see yourself through the glass.

Now add the glitter to the jar, saying:

With glitter and gold I shine so bright.
With glitter and gold I know my worth.

Hold the carnelian stone in your hand. Feel the warmth and presence of this powerful stone. Draw that feeling into your heart and say:

With carnelian I am vibrant and bold.

Hold each botanical in your hands, one by one, connecting with the special essence it holds. And add each botanical while saying:

With rose petals I am surrounded by love and kindness.
With calendula I am comforted and soothed.
With angelica I am always safe.
With hyssop I am at peace.
With bay I am crowned with light.
So shall it be.

Breathe into the jar three times and repeat your affirmation three more times. Seal the jar with the lid. Keep your jar somewhere special. Whenever you need a boost of good self-esteem, gently shake the jar and repeat your affirmation.

To Protect Your Family From Harm

Moon phase: Full Moon or Any Phase

Over the years I've worked with countless people worried about the safety and well-being of someone they love. It could be an adult with a child in an abusive relationship that they can't seem to get out of. When you are watching from the outside, wishing you could do something to help—it's one of the most disheartening feelings.

Though you can't save everyone, and sometimes your advice or support is met with silence, you can always wrap those you love in protective magic. If you find yourself in such a situation, use this spell to protect your family or a family member.

Remember, this is magic is intended to supplement the proactive steps already taken to address the issue or situation. This is a supportive measure when you feel powerless to do anything else. **Note:** This spell does not and should not take the place of professional help. Always contact the proper authorities in situations of domestic violence or abuse, or when self-harm is a possibility.

Gather together a small black box with a lid, a piece of black silk fabric twice as big as the box interior, a photo of each person you wish to protect (sans the perpetrator if they still inhabit the house), a silver marker, black tape, and the following dried botanicals: four clove buds, basil, one garlic clove, and four pieces of angelica root.

In your sacred space, ground, center, and connect with your breath. Align yourself with your desire to offer protection to your family in this difficult time.

With the silver marker write on the top of the box:

All within are protected from violence, pain, and harm.

Connect with the essence of the angelica root by holding it in your palms. Ask for this plant spirit to aid you in this endeavor by saying:

*Angelica root, protect (say the names of each person) from
harm's way.*

Place the root in the four corners of the box interior.

Connect with the essence of the basil by holding it in your palms.
Ask for this plant spirit to aid you in this endeavor by saying:

Where basil is evil cannot stay.

Place the basil in the box interior lightly covering the bottom.

Connect with the essence of the clove buds by holding them in
your palms. Ask for this plant spirit to aid you in this endeavor by saying:

Clove buds restore peace to this home.

Place one clove bud in each corner of the box.

Open the black fabric and with it line the bottom of the box, allowing
the extra length of fabric to hang over the sides (like wrapping a gift).
Now take the photos of each person, one at a time, and hold the photo
in your hand and say:

You are surrounded with protection.

Kiss the photo and place it in the center of the box.

After you've added each photo, fold the four corners of extra fabric
over the photos, covering them completely, and say:

You are surrounded with protection.

Connect with the essence of the garlic cloves by holding the bulb in
your palms. Ask for this plant spirit to aid you in this endeavor by saying:

Mighty garlic ward off all harm to the ones I love.

Break the garlic apart and add a clove to each corner of the box and place one on top of the photos wrapped in fabric. Place the cover on top of the box. Tape the lid to secure to the box and say:

All within are protected from violence, pain, and harm. So shall it be.

Hide the box in a safe place such as the back of a closet. Know that those you love are safe inside.

When You Need an Infusion of Love and Light

Moon phase: Waning or New Moon

Calendula flower-infused oil is a gentle healer for chapped and worn skin, cuts, bruises, aches and pains, and it lifts your spirit when you need some self-love and care during difficult times. Imagine this oil as a bottle of light when things feel dark and heavy. Creating this oil is easy to do and very rewarding over a lunar month.

Begin creating your oil at the Waning or New Moon because it will need to infuse for around one month. You will need a glass jar with a lid, enough dried calendula flowers to fill the jar half full, and quality olive oil.

Make sure to sterilize your jar and completely dry it before you begin. Holding the calendula flowers in your hands, connect with their essence, and say:

Calendula flowers, heal and soothe.
Bring light in darkness.

Bless with your touch.
So shall it be.

Add enough flowers to the jar to fill it half full. Then add enough olive oil to the jar to fill it to the top and say:

Olive oil, heal and soothe.
Bring light in darkness.
Bless with your touch.
So shall it be.

Breathe into the jar three times with the intention that this oil will be a soothing rub when your body, mind, and spirit need an infusion of light. Then cap the jar tightly and shake to swirl the flowers about.

Place the jar in a warm window and say:

By Sun and Moon,
Sky and time,
Infused with light,
To heal body, spirit and mind.

Shake the jar each day for a whole lunar month. After one month strain the oil through cheesecloth or a filter into a clean jar to separate the oil from the flowers. Seal tightly and keep in a cool, dark place like a cupboard.

Now when you need an infusion of light, you can use this oil to soothe your skin, massage your body, or add to a bath. You can dress a fresh white candle or a pink figure candle of your gender with the oil and light it for self-love and compassion.

Generating Prosperity and Keeping It Flowing

Moon phase: New Moon to Full Moon

Emergency money spells are great when you need them, but this spell is intended to grow your prosperity steadily over time so you have what you need when you need it.

An abundance mindset is essential to generating prosperity, wealth, and flowing finances. If you have sticky feelings about money or receiving help, take some time to work through those by doing some journaling and banishing work.

Start playing with how it feels to have the money and prosperity you need and want. Whenever something is given to you, such as a compliment, a gift, even a small amount of change, acknowledge it as a blessing. You have innumerable blessings happening every day. The Universe is filled with an endless supply of opportunities and wealth, but you have to be a welcoming home for those blessings to find you.

Find a special bowl that you will reserve for this spell. Gather all the silver change that you have in your purse, pocket, wallet, or lying around the house. Place the bowl in a windowsill on the night of a New Moon.

Add the change to this bowl and say:

As the moon increases her light, my abundance increases.
So shall it be.

Now, whenever you have spare change, add it to the bowl and know that your supply is increasing. At the Full Moon, burn a fresh green candle next to the bowl and say:

My life is filled with abundance and prosperity.
I am grateful for my ever-increasing supply.
Thank you. So shall it be.

At this time, you should take the change you've gathered since the New Moon and deposit it into your savings account. You can begin the ritual again at the next New Moon. Continue this work consistently to keep your prosperity growing and flowing.

Banishing Financial Debt

Moon phase: Waning Moon

Banishing magic is best worked during the Waning Moon. If you are dealing with financial debt, small or large, you can work this spell. To banish financial debt, you should work proactively by talking to a professional about budgeting, debt consolidation, or anything else that might help your situation. Professional advice should be your first step, and though it feels daunting, it will be the most empowering step. Smart magic is worked with best actions in mind.

Before you begin, you should know exactly what debt you owe. Calculate a dollar amount so you know exactly where you stand with the situation. Debt banishing magic is usually worked over a period of time, until the debt is gone. Alongside of working banishing magic, you can work attraction magic to draw prosperity to you.

This spell was inspired by Briana Saussy's *Money Magic & Tax Prep Mojo* discussion.

Write down the debt amount you wish to banish on a piece of paper.

Begin by smudging yourself and the space you are working in with sage. Pass the paper with the debt amount and the black candle you will use through the sage smoke and say:

Spirit of sage clears these blocks away.
Grant me the wisdom and clarity to make positive change.
So shall it be.

In a fireproof bowl burn the paper amount and say:

With knowledge and reverence I make this change.
I banish this debt from my life.
I am financially free.
Without harm. So shall it be.

Inscribe the candle with the number amount of debt you owe. Hold the candle in both hands, impressing on it your desire to banish your debt and have financial freedom. Light the candle and say:

Through sacred fire this candle melts away.
Through sacred fire my debt dwindles until gone.
I am free and clear of this burdensome weight.
Without harm. So shall it be.

Allow the candle to burn completely. Discard the ashes on a patch of earth away from your home, to be reclaimed and regenerated by nature. And, immediately after doing this ritual, make a payment on some part of your debt—no matter how small it is.

Continue this work each Waning Moon until you are free. Trust that each step you take is in the right direction. You are moving forward with knowledge and reverence. Be mindful of your expenses, ask for help when you need it, and continue to pay what debt you can.

When You Need More Business

Moon phase: New or Waxing Moon

Chamomile, with its bright and tiny daisy flowers and feathery green leaves, radiates warmth, abundance, and good energy. It smells of fresh-cut apples and sinks deep into the senses, calming the nerves and soothing the spirit. Sipping on chamomile tea is an uplifting ritual for relaxation and perfect for meditation and prayer work.

This is a very versatile herb used in many traditions, from Southern conjure to European magical systems. It carries with it a number of metaphysical and energetic associations. It's a wonderful botanical for attraction, drawing, and sweetening things.

What is interesting about chamomile is that it attracts luck and wealth energy, but it also purges negativity from your aura and surroundings. It fills you with bright, invigorating light to eradicate low vibrations and blocks that keep you from living abundantly.

Use chamomile to glow with a golden light of prosperity.

TO MAKE CHAMOMILE WASH

Infuse a large cup or pitcher with a handful of chamomile flowers or a few chamomile tea bags. When the flowers fully infuse the water, it turns a deep golden color. The aroma should fill the air and sweeten your senses.

As the water cools, visualize the infusion glowing with magnetism. Speak prayers and affirmations of wealth attraction over it. Say something from the heart, like:

Golden chamomile, shine your light upon me.
Envelop me in your warm glow of prosperity.
Draw to me wealth, good luck and business.
So shall it be.

Use this tea as a wash for the floors, walls, doors, and countertops of your business. Pour some of the tea across the threshold to your business and invite new customers and clients in.

Wash your hands and feet with this water. Or add to a full bath and soak in this golden energy. You can use this wash before a big business deal, meeting with a client, or when asking for a loan or financial favor. Some people use it before gambling.

If you run an online business or work from home, fill a spray bottle with the tea and mist your workspace. You could also keep a small bowl on your desk with chamomile flowers, a citrine crystal to pen the path to prosperity, and your business card.

Bring Peace and Harmony to a Chaotic Place

Moon phase: Any Phase

Rose water has a long history of uses from cuisine to cosmetics, and it is an invaluable tool for spiritual work. With a light and fragrant scent, rose water is a gentle spirit to bring peace and harmony to a place, to settle turbulent thoughts and feelings, and to raise the overall vibration of whatever it touches.

You can find rose water in most Mediterranean groceries or in holistic stores. Keep it on hand for whenever you need to shift the atmosphere from heavy to light. Simply mist the space with a bit of rose water, and watch the delicate scent envelop the area in a vibration of tranquility.

I find misting rose water in a room after a fight or a stressful situation keeps those energies from lingering. Whenever someone is ill or recovering from a difficult situation, rose water is a gentle way to lift their spirit. Mist your space before and after any kind of spiritual work to keep a peaceful atmosphere. Mist yourself or add rose water to your bath to enhance your aura with good vibrations.

Keep your aura or your space charged with clear intention by misting yourself or your space with rose water after smudging sage or performing another type of spiritual cleansing. You can make a practice of using rose water at the start of your day or before retiring to sleep. Keep a bottle by your bedside to help with troublesome sleep.

Mending Heartache and Grief

Moon phase: Waning Moon

Losing someone you love can throw your whole world into chaos. Whether you've lost someone to death, divorce, or some kind of ending, the experience can leave you feeling raw, vulnerable, completely exposed, and unable to move on. Sometimes the loss is sudden and shocking, giving you little time to process how you really feel in the situation. Other times, it's long and drawn out, slowly wearing down your sense of self.

Whatever your experience, being thrown into the shadows of grief and heartache is a personal journey; there's no timeline for your healing process and no one can ever truly understand what you're feeling. In this time, be gentle with yourself, listen to your body, rest when you need to, and let your loved ones support you when they can.

Use this ceremony to help ease the weight of your heartache. You will need one Apache tear. These are beautiful black obsidian stones that naturally form into rough, interestingly shaped pebbles. As gentle spirit allies, Apache tears can help you work through your loss, ground your unsettled feelings, and protect you when you're most vulnerable.

Perform this ceremony during the Waning Moon. Start by washing your special Apache tear in a small bowl of fresh milk to nourish, soothe, and awaken your connection to the stone spirit. Rinse with spring water and dry with a towel.

Take time to build a connection with your stone by sitting with it in sacred space. Close your eyes and focus on your breathing. Let yourself relax into your body, the space around you, and this moment in time.

Hold your stone and gently roll it between your fingers, over your palms, back and forth from each hand; just feel the texture of the stone's surface, craters, rough spots, and grooves. See how you feel doing this. Let yourself be open and perceptive.

Out loud or in your mind, confide in your stone. This is your chance to tell your story of loss, pain, and heartache. Tell the stone what grief weighs heavy on your heart. You can do this for as long as you like. This is a patient stone, so you can pause if you need to catch your thoughts or wipe your tears.

At some point, you will feel something move through you. A feeling of release will come over you. You might feel hot, cold, or tingly. You might sense a pressure, weight, or tension lift from you body. Just notice what happens for you.

When you feel this sense of release, thank your stone for listening and supporting you. Place your stone on your altar or in some safe place. If life is feeling really chaotic, keep your stone by your bedside. Whenever you need to release your heavy feelings or get something off your chest, hold your stone and allow it to support you.

Be kind to your stone ally. Offer a milk bath to your stone whenever it feels right. When you've reached a milestone in your personal healing journey, bury your Apache tear in the earth. If you still feel you need your stone, leave it buried for a whole lunation, then retrieve it. If you feel ready to move on, then leave your stone to rest.

Soothing an Unwell Pet

Moon phase: Full Moon or Any Phase

Pets are such special companions and often one of the most important presences in your life. I truly believe our furry friends are healers sent here to walk with us through the ups and downs of life, and often lessening the blow of our most painful experiences. When your pet is unwell, you can feel pretty helpless to ease their pain. After taking them for a proper medical visit, use this ceremony to soothe them.

When your pet is unwell, you should respect their space. Avoid making changes to your environment that might induce stress or anxiety. Animals will often sleep or rest for long periods of time if they are ill, and they may not be as friendly as usual. Try not to force affection on them, but let them know you are there to offer loving support and care.

Fresh water is essential for your pet's well-being. Use this necessity as a tool for offering them healing and soothing energies. Dedicate a special pitcher to hold fresh water for your pet.

In this pitcher, place a piece of tumbled rose quartz, clear quartz, and citrine (crystals in the quartz family are safe in water). Fill the pitcher with fresh filtered or spring water. Hold your hands over the pitcher and infuse it with intention. See, sense, and know that your pet will be soothed, supported, and healed in whatever way is beneficial for their highest good.

Speak these words over the water:

Clear quartz for vitality and strength.
Rose quartz for love and support.
Citrine for blessings of good health.
Soothing water, ease (your pet's name) pain.
So shall it be.

Use this water to fill your pet's water bowl. Clean the bowl daily and refresh the water. Avoid putting the stones directly in the water bowl! You can keep this pitcher in the refrigerator or add stones to a large water bottle.

You could also tuck these three stones into your pet's bed or someplace where they regularly sleep.

Dealing with Harassment, Bullies, and Negative People

Moon phase: Waning Moon, or Any Phase

Harassment is painful in any form. Over time, it wears down your confidence and sense of self or, worse, turns into harm. Harassment could be a daily assault, such as a negative coworker who leaves you feeling blah after every conversation, a school bully who never lets up, or a family member who forces their will upon you. On- and offline, these attacks are draining, and you don't deserve them.

For this spell you will need a clean glass jar with a lid, a bottle of white vinegar, a photo of the harasser (or write their full name on a sheet of paper), and a bulb of fresh garlic.

Place the photo or name paper of the person harassing you into the jar, and say:

> Leave me alone.
> Let me be free.
> Your harassment stops here.
> So shall it be.

Hold the garlic bulb in your hands. Connect with the essence of this powerful plant, and silently ask for its protection and power to ward off the harmful influence of your harasser. Break the blub apart, place it in the jar, and say:

> Leave me alone.
> Let me be free.

Your harassment stops here.
So shall it be.

Hold the vinegar and silently ask that it dissolve all connection you have with this person. Ask that their power and influence over you be taken away. Pour the vinegar into the jar filling it up and say:

Leave me alone.
Let me be free.
Your harassment stops here.
So shall it be.

Seal the jar tightly. Shake the jar vigorously, holding in your mind your desire to dissolve the harassment being inflicted upon you. With as much feeling as you can must, repeat these words as many times as you feel called to:

Leave me alone.
Let me be free.
Your harassment stops here.
So shall it be.

When you are finished, place the jar in a dark cabinet. Leave it there indefinitely. Let the person stew in the vinegar and garlic until it dissolves their influence completely. Should they start harassing you again, give the jar a good shake and place it back in the dark.

Honoring Someone Who Has Passed Away

Moon phase: Any Phase

Death is a precarious thing. We seldom discuss it, and when we lose some-one, there's little support for grieving the loss. There's no timeline for grief or healing. Years can pass, yet those feelings still linger. The pain of losing someone you love is something that may never truly heal. Sometimes the best way to work through those feelings is by honoring their memory.

Gather three sprigs of fresh rosemary and a spool of red yarn.

Rosemary is for remembrance. It has a long history of uses for funerary practices and honoring the dead. Red is a color of life, love, and vitality.

Cut three pieces of yarn the length of your hand. With the thread, tie a bow to the top of each rosemary sprig, and say:

Gone from the earth, but not forgotten.
Your memory is honored with thoughts and tears.
Your presence is welcomed in my life and heart.
I send love and peace wherever you are.
So shall it be.

Leave one sprig on the person's grave, or someplace that held special meaning to that person, as a sign of honor and a signal that you still treasure their memory. Leave one sprig on your altar or someplace where you will see it and think of them fondly.

Hang the last sprig to dry over the course of a lunation. Once the sprig has dried completely, burn it in a fireproof bowl and repeat the words above. At this time, you can speak from your heart, tell the person in spirit whatever you need—to make peace, to offer love, to ease your pain. They will hear your words.

For Success in Any Situation

Moon phase: Any Phase

Use this spell when you desire success in a situation, especially when you need to be eloquent, charming, and on your game! Try this before a presentation, an interview, a court case, or business venture.

On a dried bay leaf, write the word "success" with a marker. Hold the leaf and focus on your desire for success. Envision yourself in the situation, armed with all the right things, the right words, the right response, and the right outcome.

Burn the leaf in a fireproof bowl and say:

Bless this venture with success.
Bless my words with eloquence.
Bless me with favorable influence.
Bless me with crowning success.

Place the bowl at your feet and hold the burning leaf like a stick of incense. Waft the smoke from your feet upward, over your body, to your head. Bathe in the smoke and know that you are enchanted with success.

Attracting New Love into Your Life

Moon phase: Waxing Phase

Spells and magic for love have a long history and deep allure. Many seekers have begun their magical journey from the simple desire to draw a lover near. Your opinions about love magic will be guided by your own moral compass and spiritual tradition. With that being said, I never feel it wise to work love magic in a manipulative way. Instead of trying to make someone love you, why not draw from the endless supply of potential in the Universe and call a new lover to your life?

For this magical work, you will be creating a charm bag to empower yourself with love-drawing potential.

You will need a small red drawstring bag, two magnets that stick together, two rosebuds, a rose quartz crystal, two sheets of paper, a pen, a red candle, a lighter, and a bottle of your favorite perfume or perfume oil.

To begin this magical working, light the candle. Take your two sheets of paper and spend some time dreaming on the ideal lover you'd like to draw into your life.

On the first sheet of paper, make a list of the traits that you would *not* want in a person. Focus on their personality, lifestyle, and their overall perspective on the world. You can list physical traits if you want, but make sure that these are nonnegotiable things! Drawing a lover near is about attracting someone to you that matches your personality and perspective of life—but the form that person takes could surprise you!

Take your time to create this first list. Once you've finished, spend time with the list, contemplate what you've written, and ask yourself what you would desire instead. What qualities would the opposite person have? Usually we are far more capable of listing what we don't want with extreme specificity, but when it comes to listing what we *do* want, it becomes a challenge.

On your second sheet of paper, list the qualities you do want in a lover. Dream, play, and think big and small here. Consider the goals and outlooks you have on life and how a partner would fit into those aspirations.

Review your new list of ideal qualities and ask yourself, "Am I upholding those qualities in my own life?"

Setting your list aside for a day or two can be very helpful. When you are ready to come back and review the list one more time, you can rewrite it, perhaps revising the essentials. Remember, you are not mail-ordering an exact person—you're sending out an energetic signal requesting a response that matches the vibration you've identified.

With your list in hand, you are ready to construct your love-drawing charm. Gather your ingredients together in sacred space. Find time for stillness and connect with your breath. Set an intention for yourself that you are here to draw a new lover who holds all the traits and qualities you've clarified, and you are open to see how this takes form.

Begin by holding the drawstring bag in your hands and connecting with your clear desire.

Read through your list and name each thing out loud. Feel the energy and momentum build as you read the qualities. Imagine yourself calling the perfect person closer to you.

Fold your sheet of paper toward you a few times until it is a small square that fits neatly into the red bag. As you add the paper into the charm bag, saying:

I desire a new love in my life.
Bring to me the person with these qualities.
I open myself to love and new beginnings.
Surprise and delight me.
Let (him or her) come to me with ease.
With only love and good feeling.
For the highest good of all.
So shall it be.

Separate the two magnets and hold one in each hand. Focus on your desire for this person, and slowly bring the magnets together. Feel how they naturally draw toward one another. As you do this, saying:

As these magnets naturally draw to one another.
My new love is naturally drawn to me.
With only love and good feeling.
For the highest good of all.
So shall it be.

Add the magnets to the charm bag.

Hold the quartz crystal in your hand and fill it with your desire. Ask the crystal to amplify and empower your desire with pure energy. Add the crystal to the bag, saying:

My desire is clear like this quartz.
My new love finds me with ease.
Feel me, see me, know me, find me.
This crystal draws you near.

With only love and good feeling.
For the highest good of all.
So shall it be.

Take the two dry rosebuds in your hands. Imagine that these rosebuds are you and your new partner. Connect with the loving spirit of rose and ask that your partner find you. Add the two rosebuds to the bag, saying:

With these rosebuds I draw my new lover to me.
With only love and good feeling.
For the highest good of all.
So shall it be.

Hold the charm bag in your hands and feel all the power and intention you've added to it. With this charm bag, you've created a living vessel of magnetic power to call your desire into life. Blow into the bag three times to imbue it with life, and seal it shut with three knots.

Use your favorite perfume or oil to mist the bag. Then spray your pulse points and say:

I desire a new love in my life.
Bring to me the person with these qualities.
I open myself to love and new beginnings.
Surprise and delight me.
Let (him or her) come to me with ease.
With only love and good feeling.
For the highest good of all.
So shall it be.

Keep your charm bag with you. You can place it in your purse or pocket. You can keep it on your altar or next to your bedside table. Hold it often and connect with your desire to draw your new lover near. Once a week, or when you feel called to do so, spray it with a bit of perfume and repeat the words above.

Every time you dress yourself with your favorite perfume, know that you are also calling your new partner to you.

Moving Through Stuck Feelings and Heartbreak

Moon phase: Waning Moon, or Any Phase

Heartbreak can feel like a raging storm happening inside of you. Every thought is a dense, dark cloud hanging over you; every feeling a pang of thunder and lightning that shakes your core.

The best medicine for these stuck feelings is movement. So many times when we are hurting inside we fold into ourselves and hold tight to the pain. Something in us is afraid to let it out and let it go. Maybe it feels safe to hold on to our pain; maybe it's the last effort to keep old feelings alive.

But now you are ready to be free! Turn on some music that moves your body, your thoughts, and your feelings. Let yourself be free to express whatever storm is raging within you.

Jump, laugh, cry, sing, and scream into a pillow. Whatever you need, express it! If you feel inclined, you can use a drum, rattle, or tambourine. I like to play my guitar and sing as loud as I can.

Don't worry about how talented you are, what you look like, or how you sound. Just move through the experience. Do what you can with what you have; even if you're limited with mobility, you can still move through this energy.

When you feel tired and done releasing these feelings, let yourself collapse, lay down, and drift off into a healing twilight. When you wake up, you will feel renewed.

Mending Conflict with Someone

Moon phase: Full Moon

Conflict with another person is unsettling, and left unacknowledged it creeps into every area of your life until it festers into a wound. Letting your feelings out and finding closure can mend hearts, heal wounds, and give you the strength to move on in whatever way is necessary for your well-being.

The best medicine to clear the air and mend a conflict is to talk about your feelings. Sometimes facing these situations head-on isn't easy because of how uncomfortable it can seem to talk about feelings. Sometimes it might feel unsafe to truly acknowledge what you need to say. Please, consider what is best for you in this situation.

Whenever a face-to-face conversation isn't possible you can always connect with the person energetically. Telepathically connecting to a person's higher self is the best way to go about this. You are basically creating a line of communication where you can express what you need to say. On a deeper level they will hear your words, and they can choose what to do with them.

When we connect to someone on a deeper level and appeal to their higher self, we bypass the walls, shields, and filters that most of us carry as a form of protection. You are getting to the true person, rather than the person they wish you to see. Again, there is nothing manipulative or cohesive about this work—you are simply sending a message and they get to choose what comes next.

On a fresh white candle, carve the name of the person you wish to speak to. Hold this candle, and connect with your desire to speak with this person's higher self. Keep your energy soft, gentle, and inviting.

Light the candle and say:

Guiding forces gather round.
With this candle I make the call.
Through this light I send these words.
With only respect I speak these words.
(Person's name), please hear me.

Now place a photo of the person in front of the candle, close your eyes, and connect with their energy. Take a moment to make the link. You might feel them open up to you right away, or it could take some time. When you feel a click, you know you are ready to speak.

At this time, you can say whatever you need to say. Get it all off your chest. Imagine you are speaking with them face-to-face. Be open and honest, but keep a warm inviting tone. Remember, you want to mend and heal.

When you are finished, thank the person for hearing you out. Blow out the candle and know that they have heard you on some level.

Lunar Alchemy

Blessing a Community

Moon phase: Waxing Moon, or Any Phase

People face struggles every day, and as the chaos around us increases, the pain and misfortune we see is staggering. In difficult times, there's a desire to help heal and mend the pain of others. This ceremony is an act of blessing for a family, group, or community. Use this when you want to help, but don't know any other way you can.

Go on a nature walk so you can connect with the spirit of life and nature. Let your heavy heart and prayers move through you while you wander down the street or through nature. Hold in your mind and heart the individuals you wish to bless. You can think of them by name, or if it's a group of people, then think generally of all the parties involved.

As you walk, notice what is happening around you. Feel the breeze, see the animals, and take in the sounds. Begin to gather a flower for each person that you wish to bless. When you pick this flower, ask that it offer its blessing for the person in need.

Continue doing this until you've gathered a bouquet of flowers for all the people you wish to bless. When you've come to the end of your walk, take a moment to rekindle your intention. Let your desire to heal, bless, and help move through you and into this beautiful bouquet.

Leave the flowers near a tree and say a prayer from your heart that the divine spirit is with them through this experience.

Alternatively, if you are unable to go for a walk because of location or season or weather, you can purchase a bouquet. As you place each bloom in a new vase with fresh water, acknowledge the flower as a blessing upon the person in need.

Place the bouquet in a sunny window where it can bathe in warmth and light. Know that those blessings will find the people in need.

A Love Letter to Yourself

Moon phase: Any Phase

I know you feel the heaviness in the world right now. Life can feel like walls pressing in on you, caging you up tight, and locking you deep inside. But there's light in there, and it will leak through the tiniest cracks and bloom into expression.

While you're out there doing your best, just know you're not alone. Someone out there cares about you. I want to validate your feelings. I want you to know it's okay to grapple with pain—it fortifies your light. And I want you to know its okay to shine—that is your purpose.

I've never walked in your shoes. I can only know my own journey, but I know that feeling of dancing in the dark, trying to find the next glittering step forward. Let yourself be in the unknown. Keep dancing until you discover what's next. Allow yourself to be in process.

You're going through changes, and you'll keep going through changes because that is the nature of life unfolding. Sometimes I think it's easy to want to fight the process of change, to skip ahead and be on the other side of the uncertainty. Yet, the uncertainty, the unknown places that we all have to venture into, always hold the promise of possibility.

Digging your heels in the ground means slowly disappearing; it's only through forward motion that we can become transformed. But there is momentum in the stillness, and stillness in the movement.

Think about what you've done, how you've grown, and all the things you've experienced in your life so far. Each one of those experiences has brought you to this moment and helped you to discover just a fraction of who you are, and if you keep going, you will get closer and closer to your own truth. There's so much more to uncover the deeper you go.

But it's not a destination. With each step you take, the coordinates change. If you're curious, you'll discover who you are on an inner level, the constant part of you that lives under the surface, the part of you that doesn't bend, change, hide, or break depending on the situation. You will meet your most luminous self!

Fighting isn't the way forward. Life can be like a river—you can move with the current or go against it. If you fight the current, you wear yourself down until you have no fight left. Or you can move with it, see where it takes you, grow curious to each moment and allow it to fortify your inner light and your unique purpose.

And know that the Universe isn't some thing out *there*, separate from you. It's a part of you. You are one and the same. We are all unique expressions of the Universe experiencing itself. In those dark, insidious moments where you feel inflamed from the inside out, just know that you're actually discovering your inner wisdom, your soul. The light inside of you cares enough about living truth to point out to you where you are showing up small and unexpressed. Your pain becomes your teacher. Honoring your pain is honoring your wisdom.

So feel whatever you feel in this moment: the pain, the anger, the sadness, and the joy. Emotions don't have to rule your life; they can inform your journey. I think of emotions like weather. The wind, the rain, and the thunder—even the sunshine—they aren't constant, but they do show us the present moment and how easy or difficult things are or will be moving forward.

So what emotion is moving through you now?

What change is it inspiring within you?

How is it fortifying your light?

A MINI RITUAL FOR HONORING YOUR LIGHT

- Light a fresh white candle. Stare into the flame, watch it bob, dance, and spin on the wick. Let this light lull you deeper into your body and your being.

- Notice what emotions or feelings are drawn from the depths by this firelight. Just hold space for them, witness yourself in this moment. Whatever you feel . . . let it move through you.

- When you're ready, ask the question: How do I want to move forward?

- Make a declaration in this moment to do just that . . . to honor and work your light.

- Say out loud: *"And so it is."*

- Then blow out the flame.

Even when you don't see it, just know that you're amazing, you're strong, you're intelligent, and you're worthy. Let the darkness show you the way forward. And when the light cracks through, embrace it. Embrace your lucid moments of knowing exactly who you are. Just drop the act of being something, and instead be your present self. Regardless of who's watching or judging, be beautiful in this moment.

The present moment is the truth. Don't let the potential of who you can be allow you to forsake who you are right now. Own your beauty and strength, just as much as you own your darkness and pain.

The legacy of your life isn't about how popular you are or how much money you have; it's how you treat people, how you change their lives, and how much you express your own truth in the world. I think of life like art—it has no meaning other than to move something inside of us that is deep, primal, and eternal. If your life is your art, what do you want people to feel when they experience you?

If I could offer any advice, it would be to practice radical self-care, because that is the most compassionate and audacious thing you can do for yourself. And have boundaries: this means acting out of integrity and listening to what feels right in your soul. Say yes when you mean yes. Say no when you mean no. And don't be afraid to say goodbye to people, situations, and responsibilities that dim your light and no longer inspire you to be the best version of yourself.

And when it comes down to it, don't do things out of expectation or approval of others. Do things because they makes you feel exactly like the person you want to be. You don't have to do, be, act, or say anything that that isn't your truth.

Instead of listening to the outside voices, ask yourself: Do I like who or how I am showing up?

That's true integrity.

Reflection

Go out into the world and stand strong in your own power. Embrace whatever phase you are in. When you feel lost or stuck, when you feel there's nowhere else to turn, look toward the sky where the Moon is watching over you.

Let her guide you through the challenges and blessings in your life. She is a reminder that you are filled with light, with magic, and with wonder.

As my mom always says: "I am sending you love through the Moon."

—Shaheen

Resources

Moon Calendars

Make A Moon Phase Calendar and Calculator
www.jpl.nasa.gov

Moon Phase Calendar
www.calendar-12.com

Timing with the Moon
cafeastrology.com

Where to Go for Help

Crisis Text Line
www.crisistextline.org
A free resource, with trained counselors, for those struggling with anxiety, depression, suicidal thoughts, or any type of emotional crisis.

Suicide Prevention Lifeline
suicidepreventionlifeline.org
Contact to get help anytime, 24/7.

TalkSpace
www.talkspace.com
Professional help with a licensed therapist that's affordable and convenient.

Meetup
www.meetup.com
If you're feeling depressed or hopeless, please don't isolate yourself. Meetup can connect you with fellow human beings who share your same interests.

Recommended Reading

Ahlquist, Diane. *Moon Magic: Your Complete Guide to Harnessing the Mystical Energy of the Moon.* Adams Media, 2017

Antenucci, Nancy. *Psychic Tarot: Using Your Natural Psychic Abilities to Read the Cards.* Llewellyn, 2011.

Baron-Reid, Colette. *Messages From Spirit: The Extraordinary Power of Oracles, Omens, and Signs.* Hay House, 2008.

Basile, Lisa Marie. *Light Magic for Dark Times: More than 100 Spells, Rituals, and Practices for Coping in a Crisis.* Fair Winds Press, 2018.

Beck, Renee and Sydney Barbara Metrick. *The Art of Ritual: Creating and Performing Ceremonies for Growth and Change.* Apocryphile Press, 2012.

Bosnak, Robert. *A Little Course in Dreams.* Shambhala, 1998.

Cameron, Julia. *The Artist's Way.* Tarcher/Perigree, 2016.

Cheung, Theresa. *The Dream Dictionary from A to Z: The Ultimate A–Z to Interpret the Secrets of Your Dreams.* HarperCollins UK, 2006.

Chodron, Pema. *When Things Fall Apart: Heart Advice for Difficult Times.* Shambhala, 2016.

Conway, D.J. *Moon Magick: Myth & Magic, Crafts & Recipes, Rituals & Spells* Llewellyn, 2002.

Cornell, Ann Weiser. *The Radical Acceptance of Everything: Living a Focusing Life.* Calluna Press, 2005.

Cunningham, Scott. *Cunningham's Encyclopedia of Magical Herbs.* Llewellyn, 1985.

Davidson, Catherine W., Ph. D. and Ramona P. Rubio Ph. D. *The Alchemical Woman: A Handbook for Everyday Soulwork.* Cultural Tapestries, 2007.

Dial, Tabitha. *Creative Divination: Read Tea Leaves & Develop Your Personal Code.* CreateSpace, 2018.

Elliott, Carolyn. *Existential Kink: Unmask Your Shadow and Embrace Your Power.* Weiser Books, 2020.

Estés, Dr. Clarissa Pinkola. *Women Who Run With the Wolves: Myths and Stories of the Wild Woman Archetype*. Ballantine Books, 1996.

Ford, Debbie. *The Dark Side of the Light Chasers: Reclaiming Your Power, Creativity, Brilliance, and Dreams*. Riverhead Books, 2010.

Fortune, Dion. *Psychic Self-Defense*. Weiser Classics, 2020.

Gawain, Shakti. *Meditations: Creative Visualization and Meditation Exercises to Enrich Your Life*. New World Library, 2016.

Gilbert, Elizabeth. *Big Magic: Creative Living Beyond Fear*. Riverhead Books, 2016.

Goddard, Neville. *Feeling Is The Secret*. CreateSpace, 2015.

Jodorowsky, Alejandro. *Psychomagic: The Transformative Power of Shamanic Psychotherapy*. Inner Traditions, 2010.

Illes, Judika. *Magic When You Need It: 150 Spells You Can't Live Without*. Weiser Books, 2008.

James, Ursula. *Source: A Manual of Everyday Magic*. Tarcher/Perigree, 2011.

Johnson, Robert A. *Owning Your Own Shadow: Understanding the Dark Side of the Psyche*. HarperSanFrancisco, 1994.

Jung, C. G. *Collected Works, Volume 12: Psychology and Alchemy*. Princeton University Press, 1980.

Kraig, Donald Michael. *Modern Magick: Twelve Lessons in the High Magickal Arts*. Llewellyn, 2010.

The Kybalion: A Study of The Hermetic Philosophy of Ancient Egypt and Greece by The Three Initiates.

Lawrence, Lauren. *Dream Keys: Unlocking the Power of Your Unconscious Mind*. MUF Books, 2009.

Marlan, Stanton. *The Black Sun: The Alchemy and Art of Darkness*. Texas A&M University, 2008.

McCoy, Edain. *The Witch's Moon: A Collection of Lunar Magick and Rituals*. Llewellyn, 2012.

Miro, Shaheen and Theresa Reed. *Tarot for Troubled Times*. Weiser Books, 2019.

Miro, Shaheen. *The Lunar Nomad Oracle*. Weiser Books, 2018.

Myss, Caroline. *Anatomy of the Spirit: The Seven Stages of Power and Healing*. Penquin Random House, 1996.

Pamer, Kerrilynn and Cindy Diprima Morisse. *High Vibrational Beauty: Recipes & Rituals for Radical Self Care*. Rodale, 2018.

Raff, Jeffrey. *Jung and the Alchemical Imagination*. Nicholas-Hays, 2000.

Roth, Gabrielle. *Connections: The Threads of Intuitive Wisdom*. Raven, 2014.

Saussy, Briana. *Making Magic: Weaving Together the Everyday and the Extraordinary*. Sounds True, 2019.

Scheffer, Mechthild. *Bach Flower Therapy: Theory and Practice*. Healing Arts Press, 1986.

Sherman, Harold. *How to Foresee and Control Your Future*. Fawcett, 1970.

Spencer, Ezzie. *Lunar Abundance*. Running Press, 2018.

Singer, Michael A. *The Untethered Soul: The Journey Beyond Yourself*. New Harbinger Publications, 2007.

Wachter, Aidan. *Six Ways: Approaches & Entries for Practical Magic*. Red Temple Press, 2018.

Acknowledgments

A book is woven from threads of inspiration, personal experience, and the support of many beautiful souls. I want to express my gratitude for everyone who has been a part of this journey. Kathryn Sky-Peck and the rest of my Weiser family: your dedication to sharing knowledge and wisdom means the world to me. Theresa Reed: you are a pillar in my life and the Tarot community. C. G. Jung: you've given us so many ways to explore the soul. Stevie Nicks: you've taught me so much about magic. My family, blood and soul: you keep me growing

About the Author

Shaheen Miro is the creator of *The Lunar Nomad Oracle* deck, *The Uncommon Tarot* deck, and coauthor of *Tarot for Troubled Times*. He offers intuitive readings, intention setting, and energy-clearing services to clients around the world—along with magical products like aura elixirs. He writes a blog and newsletter on healing, empowerment, and transformation, and he's a columnist for *numerologist.com*. He also posts weekly Intuitive Forecasts on YouTube to help people shake off negative vibes and get prepared for a beautiful week.

His mantra is "I am open and curious about life." He loves late-night karaoke, suede platform shoes, and watching *Practical Magic* on repeat. He's a nomad and lives all over the world.

To Our Readers

Weiser Books, an imprint of Red Wheel/Weiser, publishes books across the entire spectrum of occult, esoteric, speculative, and New Age subjects. Our mission is to publish quality books that will make a difference in people's lives without advocating any one particular path or field of study. We value the integrity, originality, and depth of knowledge of our authors.

Our readers are our most important resource, and we appreciate your input, suggestions, and ideas about what you would like to see published.

Visit our website at *www.redwheelweiser.com* to learn about our upcoming books and free downloads, and be sure to go to *www.redwheelweiser.com/newsletter* to sign up for newsletters and exclusive offers.

You can also contact us at *info@rwwbooks.com* or at

Red Wheel/Weiser, LLC
65 Parker Street, Suite 7
Newburyport, MA 01950